VICTORIAN GOTHIC HOUSE STYLE

AN ARCHITECTURAL AND INTERIOR DESIGN
SOURCE BOOK

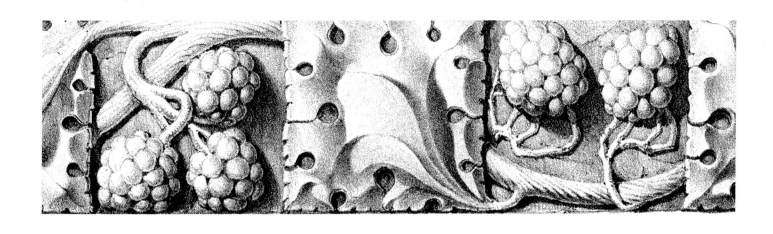

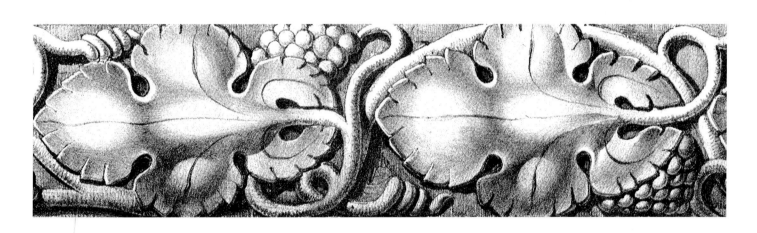

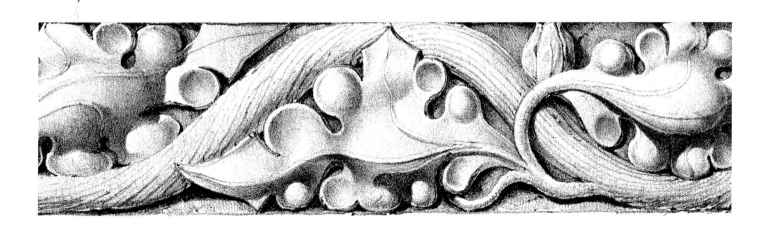

VICTORIAN GOTHIC HOUSE STYLE

AN ARCHITECTURAL AND INTERIOR DESIGN SOURCE BOOK

LINDA OSBAND

David & Charles

Contents

Introduction

'Gothic is not an art for knights and nobles; it is an art for the people: it is not an art for churches or sanctuaries; it is an art for houses and homes: it is not an art for England only, but an art for the world: above all, it is not an art of form or tradition only, but an art of vital practice and perpetual renewal. And whoever pleads for it as an ancient or formal thing, and tries to teach it you as an ecclesiastical tradition or a geometrical science, knows nothing of its essence, less than nothing of its power.'

John Ruskin

Although the Gothic Revival began in the eighteenth century, it was not until the nineteenth century that the movement reached its zenith and Gothic architecture was championed as the most important aesthetic and philosophical style to adopt. While domestic Gothic architecture of the eighteenth century was seen as picturesque and romantic – and was employed primarily by members of the aristocracy, newly interested in the medieval world, when altering their country houses or building ornamental structures in their gardens – the nineteenth-century style had a strong moral and Christian element to it, which appealed to the new, wealthy middle classes.

In England the sources of inspiration for the Gothic Revival were the ruins of the many abbeys and ecclesiastical buildings destroyed during the Dissolution of the Monasteries (1536-9), as well as the many fortified medieval castles still standing. Inspiration also came from the medieval towns and great stone cathedrals of northern France and Germany, where Gothic architecture had evolved from the middle of the twelfth century until the early sixteenth century.

Architecture in northern Europe in the Middle Ages, despite regional differences, was based on the pointed arch, the ribbed vault (an arched roof or ceiling), the gable and the flying buttress (masonry or brickwork projecting from a wall to give it additional support), and buildings were created by master-masons not architects. In England, medieval architecture is usually divided into three periods and styles: Early English, or Early Pointed, from c. 1175 (beginning with Wells Cathedral); Decorated, from c. 1300, which is characterised by the ogee (a double or S-curve occurring chiefly in arches and in the stonework around windows) and the maximum of decoration, especially of stylised foliage; and Perpendicular, from

OPPOSITE: *A detail taken from the Palace of Westminster, which displays many of the Gothic motifs used extensively by Pugin throughout the building.*

BELOW: *An example from Pugin's* Floriated Ornament *illustrating how to present natural forms as stylised, two-dimensional patterns.*

7

c. 1335, which is characterised by straight verticals and horizontals, fan vaults, colonettes (slender columns) and large windows.

There was a gradual transition from each period to the next, the key differences being in the design of the windows and the gradual development of vaulting and buttressing, where the thick walls, barrel-vaults, flat buttresses and narrow windows of the early thirteenth century were replaced by larger buttresses with thinner walls between them, thinner vaults supported on stone ribs, and larger windows filled with tracery (decorated, pierced stonework at the head of a window).

The interiors of Gothic cathedrals are characterised by a series of colonettes rising from the nave piers to the start of the vaulted ceiling, which give the length of the church the sense of soaring vertical lines. The load-bearing ribs not only take the weight of the building but also support the roof. Therefore, with the vaulting holding up the roof, the masonry walls were no longer needed for support and were soon cut away as much as possible, leaving a large interior space. In between the colonettes, windows were gradually added, so that the walls appeared to be made of glass, as, for example, in King's College Chapel, Cambridge (1446-1515) and Henry VII's Chapel at Westminster Abbey (1503-19).

The use of light through these large panes of glass — often pierced and glazed with beautiful stained glass depicting religious subjects — was an important feature of late Gothic architecture as it was seen to symbolise the glow of 'heavenly spiritual light'.

By the sixteenth century, however, the religious and cultural orders of the medieval world were disintegrating. With the rediscovery of the writings of Vitruvius (first century BC) and his *Five Orders of Greek and Roman Columns,* and a revived interest in the language of Classical architecture – its symmetry, columns, pediments and rounded arches – and the wonders of Greek and Roman civilisation, Renaissance architects developed a style that was deemed superior to others, and branded medieval architecture as 'barbaric'. The style held sway for the next three hundred years.

The word 'Gothic' was first attached to the architecture of the Middle Ages by Giorgio Vasari in his *Lives of the Most Eminent Architects, Painters and Sculptors* (1550), when he attributed it to the descendants of the Goths, a 'savage' Teutonic people who sacked Rome in 410. As he wrote disparagingly, this style of architecture was 'very different in its proportions and its decorations from both the antique and the modern. Its characteristics are not adopted these days by any of the leading architects, who consider them monstrous and barbaric, wholly ignorant of the accepted ideas of sense and order.' Although Vasari was historically inaccurate in his observations, his name for this style of architecture stuck.

However, Gothic architecture did not vanish altogether over the next two centuries. It was still seen as appropriate for certain types of buildings, especially cathedrals like Orléans and Milan and the rebuilding of Oriel and University Colleges, Oxford, and St John's College Library, Cambridge. Although primarily used for ecclesiastical buildings, Gothic tracery and decoration was still found on houses of the wealthy in medieval Europe as well as on many French châteaux, especially in the Loire Valley. In England many fortified houses were built with Gothic features and oriel windows (small projecting bays on an upper storey of a building supported underneath by decorated brackets of timber or stone), often inset with tracery. Masons and workshops specialising in Gothic architecture continued to flourish as existing buildings needed to be restored and enlarged, and specialist knowledge was passed on from master to apprentice. However, by the mid-seventeenth century this knowledge had diminished and Gothic was seen as an appropriate form of architecture only when used to renovate or extend an existing medieval building.

The first group of buildings of the eighteenth-century Gothic Revival were ornamental garden structures – medieval-looking summerhouses, temples and sham ruins – designed to create a vista or enhance a view. With the growth in the importance of landscape gardening and the publication of Batty Langley's *Ancient Architecture Restored and Improved* (1741-2), this 'new' style of architecture – Gothick – was soon being more widely adopted for small country houses and villas, as well as for larger houses and castles based on sites with medieval associations.

OPPOSITE*: The Medieval Court at the Great Exhibition, 1851, which the editor of the* Art-Journal Catalogue *called 'one of the most striking portions of the Exhibition'.*

LEFT*: The Grand Drawing Room at Fonthill Abbey, William Beckford's romantic Gothic folly. Its architectural and interior features were inspired by medieval sources.*

The first house to be wholly built in the Gothic Revival style was Strawberry Hill at Twickenham (1750-63). Its owner, Horace Walpole (1717-97), was the author of the first Gothic novel, *The Castle of Otranto*, which inspired later writers such as Sir Walter Scott. Walpole was determined to create a 'little Gothic castle', and to achieve this he based his designs on antiquarian illustrations, details from medieval buildings and his own large collection of antiquities and armour. Strawberry Hill – with its asymmetrical exterior, its battlemented roofline, crocketed pinnacles and quatrefoil windows, as well as its glittering interior decoration full of papier mâché fan-vaulting, traceried bookcases, shining weaponry and specially designed furniture – became a landmark building in the Gothic Revival which seriously challenged neo-Classicism as the prevailing style of architecture.

William Beckford's Gothic folly, Fonthill Abbey in Wiltshire, designed by James Wyatt, and Walter Scott's house at Abbotsford in Scotland were also influential in reviving interest in Gothic architecture, as was the restoration of Henry VII's Chapel and the expanding market in medieval antiquities, which found their way to Britain from Europe, in upheaval after the French Revolution and later the Napoleonic Wars.

By 1833, J. C. Loudon, author of the *Encyclopaedia of Cottage, Farm and Villa Architecture*, was declaring that, apart from the Greek and Louis XIV styles, the only other acceptable forms for furniture design were the Gothic, or Perpendicular, 'which imitates the lines and angles of Tudor Gothic architecture', and the Elizabethan, 'which combines the Gothic with the Roman or Italian manner'. His book's support for the Gothic form was not only to inspire the middle-class market but also to take the Gothic Revival to America.

The Victorian Gothic Revivalists

The man who radically transformed the Gothic Revival movement in the early years of Queen Victoria's reign (1837-1901) was Augustus Welby Northmore Pugin, who also exerted the most influence on the development of architecture and design both in England and America throughout the rest of the nineteenth century. Through his writings and architectural projects, which confirmed his belief that Gothic was the only true style to be adopted for public and domestic buildings alike, and which called for a revival of the traditional skills of medieval craftsmen, he gave architecture a new, moral stance. As Kenneth Clark wrote in his book *The Gothic Revival* (1928), Pugin laid the two foundation stones that dominated nineteenth-century art criticism and were later immortalised by John Ruskin in the *Seven Lamps of Architecture*: 'the value of a building depends on the moral work of its creator; and a building has a moral value independent of, and more important than, its aesthetic value'.

Pugin's commissions, and those of the other architects who dominated the Victorian Gothic Revival, were primarily for important public works, ecclesiastical buildings and large private mansions and country houses. However, their style was soon being adopted for smaller houses and villas, estate workers' cottages and parsonages; and although Gothic architecture was not deemed appropriate for rows of terraced houses, individual Gothic design features and motifs quickly found their way on to their façades. Local builders catering for the growing demand for housing from the expanding wealthy middle classes copied and adapted architectural plans for Gothic villas from the large number of pattern books being published, and thus completely changed the face of suburban architecture.

Although they did not design much domestic architecture themselves, the influence that the leading protagonists of the Victorian Gothic Revival had was so significant that it is important to discuss a few of them in more detail.

A. W. N. Pugin (1812-52)

Pugin was the son of a French Catholic émigré, Auguste Charles Pugin, and an English Protestant, Catherine Welby. Pugin's father, who had worked as a draughtsman for the Crown architect John Nash, was an expert on medieval Gothic detail and had published two volumes on *Specimens of Gothic Architecture* in 1821 and 1823, followed by *Gothic Furniture* (1827) and *Gothic Ornaments, Selected from Various Buildings in England and France* (1831).

Pugin grew up surrounded by drawings and books on Gothic architecture, as well as his father's large collection of medieval artefacts. He often accompanied

OPPOSITE: *The library at Strawberry Hill (1753-4), whose interior was based on illustrations of Gothic architecture and monuments from Walpole's large collection of antiquarian books and manuscripts. The bookcases echoed details taken from a print of the Gothic St Paul's Cathedral, which burnt down in the Great Fire of 1666.*

LEFT: *The drawing room at Eastnor Castle, Herefordshire, which was designed by Pugin between 1846 and 1850. The brass chandeliers were made to his design by John Hardman, while J.G. Crace executed the painting of the genealogical tree above the fireplace.*

BELOW: The frontispiece to Pugin's The True Principles of Pointed or Christian Architecture, *showing Pugin seated at a carved desk with a lectern displaying his collection of illuminated manuscripts.*

OPPOSITE: An elaborately decorated sideboard designed by Pugin and made by Crace, which was described by Christopher Dresser in the Technical Educator *as being 'carved in excess'.*

of the Anglican Church, a controversial position to take at a time when full legal rights for Catholics had only just been introduced. As a result of the subsequent demand for new Catholic churches, Pugin received a number of architectural commissions. More importantly, his conversion led him to link architecture inextricably to the Catholic Church, in the belief that Catholicism was 'the only true [Church], and the only one in which the grand and sublime style of architecture can ever be restored'. For Pugin, it was the religious faith of the master-masons that had produced the soaring wonders of the ecclesiastical buildings of the Middle Ages, and he proclaimed this in his book *Contrasts; or a Parallel Between the Noble Edifices of the Fourteenth and Fifteenth Centuries and Similar Buildings of the Present Day* (1836), in which he denounced the predominant style of neo-Classicism as 'degraded' and 'pagan'. He could see no 'reason in the world why noble cities, combining all possible convenience of drainage, water-courses and conveyance of gas, may not be erected in the most consistent and yet Christian character', and believed that a return to the principles of medieval Gothic architecture – not just its decorative forms – was a religious and moral necessity.

Another key event occurred in 1835. Pugin was invited to work for Charles Barry on the new Palace of Westminster, which was being rebuilt in the Gothic style after the Houses of Parliament had virtually been destroyed in a fire on 16 October 1834. Appointed the designer in charge of the interiors, Pugin was to spend a large part of his remaining years designing every internal feature, from the carved oak woodwork and furniture to the wallpapers, carpets, tiles, textiles, stained glass, metalwork, light fittings and ceiling decorations and mouldings, all influenced by the Perpendicular Gothic style of the fifteenth century. To help him carry out this monumental task, Pugin assembled a team of craftsmen and manufacturers, who not only interpreted his sketches into finished designs but also trained a growing number of apprentices in ancient arts and skills. This emphasis on the work of the individual in an age increasingly dependent on mass production was to have a profound impact on architects and designers, especially those who formed the Arts and Crafts movement later in the century. These specialists also produced interior furnishings, vestments and religious objects designed by Pugin for his ecclesiastical commissions.

Pugin's two basic rules of design were set out in his book *The True Principles of Pointed or Christian Architecture*, which was published in 1841. Firstly, 'there should be no features about a building which are not necessary for convenience, construction or propriety'; and secondly, 'all ornament should consist of enrichment of the essential construction of the building'. For Pugin, the architectural truth of medieval buildings in which

his father on his travels to view Gothic buildings, and by the age of fifteen, was himself designing a range of Gothic-style furniture for King George IV's apartments at Windsor. Like his father, Pugin soon became an avid collector of antiquarian objects and they were a major source of inspiration for his work.

The year 1834 was a turning-point in Pugin's life, when, after the death of his mother, he converted to Roman Catholicism. He soon became an outspoken critic the structural forms were clearly visible was all-important. To him, a building had to express the purpose for which it was designed, and he insisted on honesty in the structure and function of a building and in the materials used in its construction. This was a radical departure from the 'sham' façades of neo-Classical architecture, whose symmetry concealed a building's natural forms, and the decorative, romantic features found on eighteenth-century Gothick houses. As he later wrote in *An Apology for the Revival of Christian Architecture* (1843), 'Every building that is treated naturally, without disguise or concealment, cannot fail to look well.'

In *The True Principles*, Pugin also pronounced that flat surfaces – i.e. walls and floors – should be decorated only with two-dimensional patterns like those found in the designs of the Middle Ages, and he denounced as dishonest the three-dimensional perspectives that had been so fashionable since the Renaissance. In 1849 he developed this argument in his book *Floriated Ornament*, which called for a return to 'first principles' and the use of stylised natural forms for flowers and foliage rather than fictitious 'realistic' ones. As he wrote: 'It is ... absurd to talk of *Gothic* foliage. The foliage is natural, and it is the adaptation and disposition of it which stamps the style. The great difference between antient and modern artists in their adaptation of nature for decorative purposes, is as follows. The former disposed the leaves and flowers of which their design was composed into geometrical forms and figures, carefully arranging the stems and component parts so as to *fill up* the space they were intended to enrich ... [while] a modern painter would endeavour to give a fictitious idea of relief, as if *bunches* of flowers were laid on ...' This principle had a revolutionary effect on all aspects of interior design, especially on the work of William Morris and other members of the Arts and Crafts movement.

Apart from the houses he built for himself and his family – St Marie's Grange at Alderbury and then The Grange at Ramsgate – Pugin's few domestic commissions were from wealthy Catholic patrons who employed him to remodel existing buildings. In 1837 he received his first important commission at Scarisbrick Hall, Lancashire, the ancestral home of Charles Scarisbrick, who wanted the house altered in the Gothic style. At first only minor additions of buttresses, pinnacles, chimneystacks and an oriel window were made to the façade, but Pugin's major contribution was the building of the great hall, which included two-storey screens of carved woodwork, incorporating many early Flemish carvings from the fifteenth to the seventeenth centuries; bay windows with richly moulded arches; and an unusual mosaic floor.

Other commissions followed to remodel parts of Taymouth Castle and Alton Towers in the Gothic style,

as well as to build the Bishop's House in Birmingham. For this and for other presbyteries, Pugin chose the Flemish or North German style 'of pointed architecture because it is both cheap and effective and likewise because it is totally different from any *protestant* erection'. These buildings had very little decoration and 'exhibited a solid solemn and scholastic character that bespoke them at once to be the habitations of men who were removed far beyond the ordinary pursuits of life'.

Interest in the Gothic style became more widespread after the Chamber of the House of Lords opened in 1847 and soon became the most influential interior of its day. The Gothic cause also reached a wider audience through the Medieval Court at the Great Exhibition in 1851, which was held in the Crystal Palace in Hyde Park. Pugin masterminded the display with the help of the colleagues who had produced all the decorative arts he had designed: John Hardman, Herbert Minton, J. G. Crace and George Myers. Their work received much acclaim, the *Illustrated London News* calling it 'the most unique and best harmonised display of art and skill – art in the artist and skill in the executant ... [Pugin] has marvellously fulfilled his own intention of demonstrating the applicability of Medieval art in all its richness and variety to the uses of the present day.'

Unfortunately less than a year later, in February 1852, Pugin suffered a breakdown in his health and on 14 September he died. After his death, his friends, disciples and his eldest son, Edward, continued his work and developed the Gothic Revival in a style of which he would have approved.

ABOVE: *The Midland Grand Hotel at St Pancras Station, London, George Gilbert Scott's masterpiece of Victorian Gothic architecture.*

OPPOSITE: *The extraordinary fireplace in the banqueting hall at Cardiff Castle, designed by William Burges c.1875, depicting a medieval castle.*

George Gilbert Scott (1811-78)

Scott was the son of a clergyman and was involved at an early age in the Ecclesiology Society, set up in 1836 to promote Gothic architecture in church-building and to reform ritual in the Anglican Church. When Scott first read Pugin's books, he was so inspired – exclaiming that he had been 'awakened from my slumbers by the thunder of Pugin's writings' – that he devoted the rest of his life to the revival of Gothic architecture.

Some early church commissions led him to Hamburg, where in 1844 he won the competition to restore the church of St Nicholas. After this success, he was invited to restore some of England's great cathedrals, starting with Ely Cathedral in 1847. However, it was in the field of domestic and secular architecture that Scott had most influence, as, being neither a Catholic nor a medievalist, he was not constrained by Pugin's principles. In his *Remarks on Secular and Domestic Architecture, Present and Future* (1857), Scott called for an adaptation of Gothic so that it could be used 'so freely that it will eventually become a new style – the modern style. Mullioned windows, pointed arches and high-pitched roofs can be dropped, if inconvenient, without sacrificing the true character of Gothic.' This liberation from the strict rules laid down by Pugin had an enormous impact on later Gothic Revival architects and designers.

The output of Scott's architectural practice was vast, but the two secular buildings for which he is most famous are the Midland Grand Hotel (1868-77) at London's St Pancras railway station, and the Albert Memorial (1862-72). The Midland Hotel, built of red brick with terracotta and buff-coloured stone, combined the features of thirteenth-century French Gothic architecture with an iron structure that utilised the very latest technology. The Albert Memorial, for which Scott won the design competition after the death of Prince Albert in 1861, is the epitome of High Victorian Gothic, with its golden figure of the prince, its sculptured figures, its mosaics in the gables and its glistening spire studded with glass jewels.

John Ruskin (1819-1900)

Ruskin was one of the towering figures of nineteenth-century intellectual life and, as a practising Christian and socialist, was an outspoken critic of Victorian society. An only child, born in London to wealthy, middle-class parents, Ruskin suffered an unusually strict upbringing, with its emphasis on culture, nature and moral high-mindedness.

He became widely known in 1843 when the first volume of his book *Modern Painters* was published; in it he came to the defence of J. M. W. Turner, whose Romantic paintings had been attacked by members of the artistic establishment, and heralded Turner as the leading landscape painter of the day.

In 1849 Ruskin wrote his first book on architecture, *The Seven Lamps of Architecture*. The lamps – Sacrifice, Truth, Power, Beauty, Life, Memory and Obedience – expressed his belief in the ethical and moral nature of architecture, which, he wrote, was 'the embodiment of the Polity, Life, History, and Religious Faith of nations'. This became an important tract in the literature of the Gothic Revival because, as he declared in the second edition of the book, 'the only style proper for modern Northern work is the Northern Gothic of the thirteenth century, as exemplified in England, pre-eminently by the cathedrals of Lincoln and Wells, and in France by those of Paris, Amiens, Chartres, etc. ... In this style let us build the church, the palace and the cottage; but chiefly let us use it for civil and domestic buildings.'

These beliefs were expanded in his most important book, *The Stones of Venice* (1853), in which he praised Gothic architecture for 'the magnificent science of its structure, and the sacredness of its expression'. Having studied the beauties of Venice, especially St Mark's Cathedral and the Doge's Palace, Ruskin extolled not only the wonders of medieval construction methods but also the spirituality of Gothic design.

To him, these were the result of the freedom that the craftsmen and masons of the Middle Ages enjoyed when practising their arts, which contrasted starkly with the way that factory workers had become enslaved by the repetitive techniques of mass-production since the Industrial Revolution. Medieval builders were able to express their individuality, and even if their ornament and carving at times appeared crude, their work had a vibrant quality, which Ruskin thought was far superior to anything that was being made in his own day. Creative 'freedom, humility, joy – these were the conditions in which Gothic ornament was produced,' he proclaimed. Ruskin believed that it was the savageness of Gothic craftsmanship that was the key to its dynamic energy, and he deplored the static uniformity of modern, neo-Classical design, with its perfect symmetry and 'accurate mouldings'.

The impact of *The Stones of Venice* was felt in the political debate about morality in Victorian architecture and society as a whole. Moreover, by its praise for the beauty of Italian polychromatic (multi-coloured brickwork) architecture and the promotion of the use of natural, carved forms of ornamentation, it also had a far-reaching influence on Victorian buildings. These styles of decoration were adopted by William Butterfield (1814-1900) and George Edmund Street (1824-81), two Gothic Revival architects, whose buildings displayed some of the finest examples of polychromy in England.

Ruskin's strong feeling for nature, which he said should form the basis of all ornament, and his call for honesty in art, significantly contributed to the reform of Victorian design in the second half of the century. These principles led him to support the newly formed Pre-Raphaelite Brotherhood, which in the mid-1850s was being severely criticised. They also inspired the later formation of artistic guilds and societies founded by members of the Arts and Crafts movement.

William Burges (1827-81)

Although Burges adopted the Gothic style for visual and romantic reasons, not for religious or moral ones, he was a keen medievalist, collector of antiquities and, surprisingly, a great follower of Pugin.

A talented draughtsman, Burges trained and worked as an architect, and in the 1840s and 1850s he developed his knowledge of medieval metalwork and decorative arts. At the same time he travelled extensively to Italy, France, Greece and Turkey, where he was inspired by the architecture of the Middle Ages. In 1867 he visited the Château Pierreford in Picardy, which was being restored by the great French Gothic Revivalist Eugène

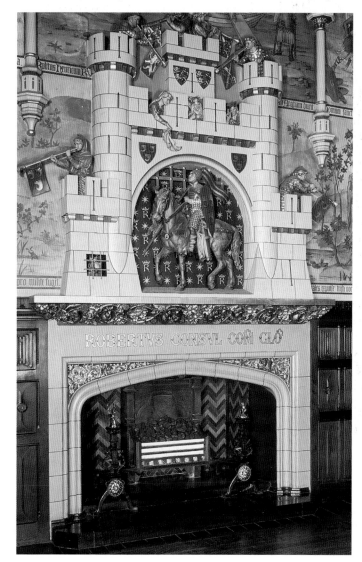

Viollet-le-Duc (1814-79), who was also responsible for renovating Sainte Chapelle and Notre Dame Cathedral in Paris, both supreme examples of thirteenth-century Gothic architecture. Like Pugin, Viollet-le-Duc believed that function was the starting-point of design, but he applied it to the new materials being introduced in the nineteenth century, especially cast iron. His highly decorative style – which was being copied at the fairy-

tale castle of Neuschwanstein then being built for Ludwig II of Bavaria – soon found expression in Burges's fantastic designs for his wealthy patron, the third Marquess of Bute. As Burges admitted, 'We all cribbed from Viollet.'

Little of Burges's work still exists, but Cardiff Castle and nearby Castell Coch, which he designed for Bute, and his own home, Tower House in Melbury Road, London, are testament to his extraordinary imagination and artistic skill. In 1868, Bute employed Burges to transform his medieval castle at Cardiff into a Gothic fantasy, a commission that took nearly twenty years to finish. The walled fortress exterior gives no hint of the exuberant, colourful interiors, which are filled with highly decorative stone and plasterwork, gilded woodwork, tiles, metalwork and stencilled patterns. Mermaids and knights, fish and monkeys, signs of the zodiac, allegorical images and winged gods decorate chimneypieces, washstands and metalwork, while gilded latticework shutters, gilded iron balconies, huge gold chandeliers, one in the shape of the sun's rays with a golden Apollo at its centre, friezes of glazed tiles of mythological scenes, a tiled floor with a map of the world in the middle, and stylised, painted furniture, all combine in the castle's splendid rooms to provide a dazzling array of colour and spectacle.

The Tower House was completed in 1878 and each room was decorated to a different theme. Again, fantastic allegorical scenes appear, expressing both

ABOVE: An illustration of a doorway at the cathedral at Lisieux, taken from Ruskin's work The Seven Lamps of Architecture.

RIGHT: William Burges's London home, the Tower House. Its round staircase tower with lancet windows, steep roof and weathervane is characteristic of many Victorian Gothic houses.

LEFT: *A design for a gatehouse in the Gothic style taken from Samuel Sloan's* The Model Architect, *one of many Victorian pattern books which influenced housebuilders across England and America.*

Burges's sense of fun and his deep knowledge of Gothic forms. Many of his allusions and stylistic designs and his bold use of colour were inspired by his study of illuminations found in medieval manuscripts.

For Castell Coch, one of Bute's summer residences, Burges created an enchanting interior, but he died in 1881 before work had barely begun. His highly decorative schemes were therefore carried out by his ex-assistant, William Frame, and the castle's unique pieces of furniture were made by John Starling Chapple, who had worked faithfully with Burges since 1859.

As Burges's extravagant work demanded wealthy patrons and took years to execute, his influence was limited, although the rare pieces of his furniture and other decorative items that reach the open market today are sought-after collectors' items. However, his importance is unquestionable, and he succeeded in dispelling the high moral tone with which Gothic Revival architecture had been imbued without sacrificing the authenticity of his sources.

The Gothic Revival in America

Loudon's *Encyclopaedia* was one of the first to inspire the Gothic Revival movement for domestic housing in the United States. With an increasing number of prosperous settlers wanting to build houses appropriate to their new status, a growing market for architectural design books was established, and their house patterns were soon being copied and developed by home-grown American architects and builders. Two of these were the landscape designer Andrew Jackson Downing (1815-52) and his partner, the New York architect Alexander Jackson Davis (1803-92). Downing's *Cottage Residences* (1841) and Davis's *Rural Residences* (1838) quickly became the standard handbooks of the American Picturesque and led to the building of Gothic Revival villas right across America.

Downing advocated rural Gothic as his preferred style of architecture for the domestic villa. In *The Architecture of Country Houses* written in 1850, he developed his philosophy for the ideal American way of life, and prescribed the most appropriate and satisfactory houses and furnishings in which he felt his fellow Americans should live. In his view, the Gothic Revival movement was the only suitable style of architecture for the pioneering spirit prevalent in America at the time, and Picturesque villas being the right kind of housing for men of imagination and energy. His house patterns for cottages and villas for people of all incomes, from the wealthy to modest farmers and clergymen, were soon being used as models by builders and architects who readily adopted his designs.

Davis is credited with designing the first Rural Gothic villa, Glen Ellen, in 1832 and, among other commissions, he went on to build two of the most important Gothic houses in the New York area: Knoll (later known as Lyndhurst) in 1838 and Kenwood in 1842. Another important architect was the British-born Richard Upjohn, who designed Oaklands, a stone castellated house in Maine, in 1835 and, most famously, a Picturesque house at Newport, Rhode Island, in 1839. His book *Rural Architecture* (1852) showed how a British Gothic villa could be built using American materials, and provided simple plans for local house-builders to follow.

Reformed Gothic

Charles Eastlake's *Hints on Household Taste* and Bruce James Talbert's *Gothic Forms Applied to Furniture, Metalwork and Decoration for Domestic Purposes*, both published in 1868, also spread the Gothic style, and their ideas were taken up by manufacturers and mass-produced, becoming very fashionable with the discerning middle classes by the 1870s. Their books were also well known in America, and by the time of the Philadelphia Centennial Exhibition in 1876, 'Modern Gothic' was at the height of its popularity.

The Reformed Gothic designers of the 1860s and 1870s – Talbert, Richard Norman Shaw, Philip Webb and William Morris – who had all either worked with George Street or been influenced by him – used simple medieval forms but in a bolder way. Medieval references were still apparent, but much of the ornament had been stripped down, leaving a more primitive but powerful appearance. By developing these designs – and looking to new sources of inspiration like Japan – these architects were soon to found the Arts and Crafts and the Queen Anne Revival movements. As a result, by the end of the century the Gothic style was on the wane for domestic housing, overtaken by these new styles on which it had had such an influence.

Chapter 1
The Plan & Façade

'My house ... is in every part a compleat building of the 15th cent. The minutest details have been attended to and the whole effect is very good ... the great thickness of the walls ... the approach over a drawbridge, the chapel with its belfry, the antient letters worked in bricks in the walls, the gilt vanes on the roof, and the small windows have astonished people about here beyond measure.'

Pugin writing about his new house,
St Marie's Grange, Alderbury, Wiltshire, 17 July 1835

OPPOSITE: *The exterior of a house in Holly Village, a Gothic Revival estate built in north London in 1865 by the philanthropist Baroness Burdett-Coutts. The architect, Henry Astley Derbishire, incorporated many Gothic features into the façade, including pointed arches, decorative brickwork, carved wooden gables, lancet windows and square towers.*

The façades of Victorian Gothic town houses and country villas were very different from the style that predominated in the 1830s at the start of the Victorian era. Asymmetrical exteriors, steeply pitched roofs, pointed arches, decorated brick and carved stonework, lancet and oriel windows, turrets, towers, campaniles, spires and weathervanes dramatically challenged the prevailing fashion for elegant, Italianate buildings with classical features, symmetrical plans, white stucco façades and roofs hidden from street view behind parapet walls.

The inspiration for this style came from the medieval architecture of northern Europe, the great cathedrals and ecclesiastical buildings and continental streetscapes with their high, sloping roofs, which were so necessary in the wetter climates of the North. Roofs like these were certainly more suited to British weather conditions than the flatter roofs, with their centre-valley rainwater gulleys, that appeared on most Georgian and early Victorian houses. As Ruskin wrote, extolling the charm of these continental houses: 'In the Netherlands, and Northern France, where material for building is brick or stone, the fronts of the stone gables are raised above the roofs, and you have magnificent and grotesque ranges of steps or curves decorated with various ornaments, succeeding one another in endless perspective along the streets ... In Picardy and Normandy, again, and many towns of Germany, where the material for building is principally wood, the roof is made to project over the gables, fringed with a beautifully carved cornice and casting a broad shadow down the house front ... But in all cases, the effect of the whole street depends upon the prominence of the gables; not only of the fronts towards the streets, but of the sides

ABOVE: *A house in the United States displaying some typical features of American Gothic buildings: an asymmetrical plan, a steeply pitched roof with a weathervane on top, intricately carved bargeboards, and a veranda extending along the outside to shield the inhabitants from the sun.*

also, set with small garret or dormer windows, each of the most fantastic and beautiful form, and crowned with a little spire or pinnacle …'

Pugin rejected the Picturesque decoration that was to be found on eighteenth-century Gothick houses and advocated a purer, more austere form of architecture. For him, the same rules applied for both domestic and ecclesiastical architecture. He believed that all parts of a house should express their function and that they should not be 'masked or concealed under one monotonous front, but by their variety in form and outline increasing the effect of the building'. Buildings should be irregular because

the variety of functions that had to be catered for could not naturally be incorporated into a symmetrical plan.

Pugin's basic rules of architecture were later widely adopted – and adapted – by architects of smaller houses and parsonages. A great critic of the use of stucco on the façades of houses – he believed it to be a 'sham' and derided 'the resistless torrent of Roman-cement men, who buy their ornaments by the yard and their capitals by the ton' – Pugin pioneered the use of red brick (with stone dressings) on his house, St Marie's Grange in Wiltshire, an unusual material in the mid-1830s. He also saw no reason why brick, a natural, 'honest' material, should not be used for town houses. With the

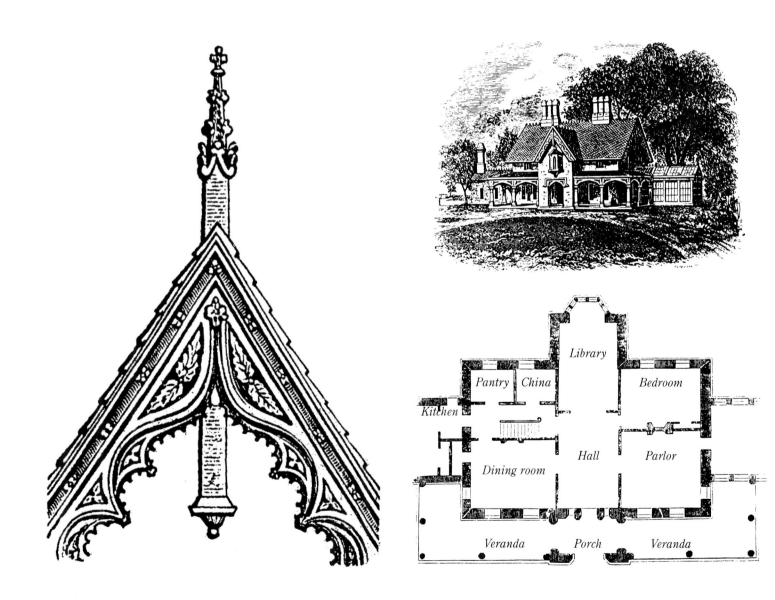

repeal of the brick tax in 1850, the brick-making industry expanded and bricks became cheaper, so that Gothic architects inspired by Pugin could build with a material that lasted longer, cost less and, with the use of different coloured bricks, formed an integral part of the structure as well as adding a decorative feature.

This decorative brickwork was developed in the 1850s and 1860s by architects and writers like John Ruskin, William Butterfield and George Edmund Street, who, inspired by buildings in Italy – especially in Venice and Verona – advocated the use of polychromy in architecture. By combining a variety of materials on the exteriors of buildings, such as contrasting coloured bricks, coloured marble and stone, bold, two-dimensional patterned façades could be designed. Butterfield's All Saints' Church, Margaret Street, London, pioneered this polychromatic brickwork and showed the dramatic effects that could be achieved. Street, who had studied the Early Christian and Islamic architecture of medieval Spain as well as that of France and Germany, also introduced more geometric forms into his designs. Soon decorative brickwork, especially layers of red and grey brick, was being copied by ordinary builders and adorned the façades of many of the thousands of suburban homes that were being constructed in the second half of the nineteenth

Downing believed that Gothic Revival, or Pointed, architecture was the ideal style for rural country houses or villas. In his books, he suggested a number of house designs, including those shown here, with gables embellished by elaborate bargeboards (opposite left).

Gothic Revival architects, inspired by the beauty of Italian polychromatic brickwork, introduced patterned brickwork to the façades of their buildings. Soon a variety of decorative brickwork appeared on the exteriors of many Victorian suburban houses.

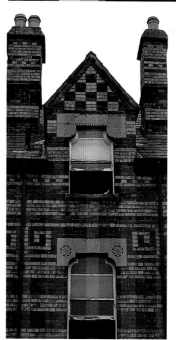

century. Flat patterns were an economical form of decoration particularly well suited to smaller houses.

The publication of Ruskin's *The Stones of Venice* in 1851 popularised the carving of foliage in stone, and his design for the Museum of Science in Oxford also incorporated elaborately carved capitals. This rediscovery of the beauty of carved stonework coincided with improved costs of quarrying and methods of transport, and thanks to the wider availability of cheaper stone, many ordinary terraced houses now had bay windows and porches decorated with capitals of stone – or mass-produced artificial stone.

After Ruskin's The Stones of Venice *was published, stone capitals, elaborately carved with foliage, flowers and other Gothic motifs, were soon to be found adding ornament to even a modest Victorian home. Drawings of medieval church architecture, such as those published in Pugin's* Gothic Ornament *and R. Glazier's* A Manual of Historic Ornament *(right and far right), provided architects and builders with authentic references on which to base their designs.*

EARLY GOTH-IC.

MIDDLE GOTHIC.

LATE GOTHIC

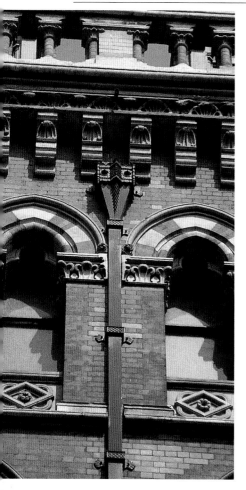

The façades of many Victorian Gothic houses were richly embellished with medieval features recreated by the expanding number of craftsmen and masons who were being trained in the ancient skills. Ornately carved stonework was placed at the top of rainwater heads and on columns as well as within Gothic arches framing windows and doors.

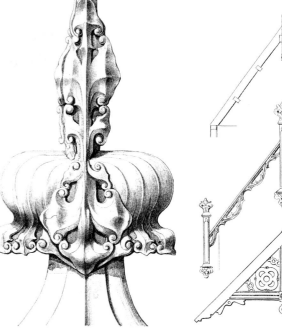

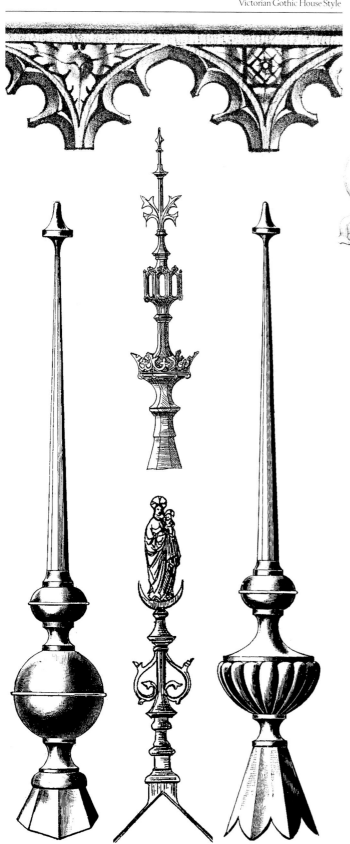

Other external features that were advocated by Pugin were steep, usually grey (Welsh) slate roofs, surmounted by cresting, finials, crockets (a small, curled, leaf-shaped ornament, which had originally appeared on Gothic cathedrals) and weathervanes; a clock tower, shown on his 1836 drawing for the new entrance façade at Scarisbrick Hall in Lancashire, which is believed to be the prototype for Big Ben at the Houses of Parliament; staircase towers, often topped by square battlements; varying styles of windows on a single building, including mullioned, bay and dormer windows, often of stained glass held within delicate stone tracery displaying trefoil or quatrefoil motifs; and prominent chimney-stacks, which became a major feature of his domestic architecture. Chimney-stacks were included for practical reasons – 'the gain of space, added stability, and avoidance of fires in the roofs' – as well as aesthetic, because a 'great variety of light and shadow, and a succession of bold features are gained in the building'.

The steeply pitched or vertical mansard roofs on Gothic Revival buildings were also seen by later architects as areas where decoration could be applied, and contrasting bands of different tones of slate, sometimes inset with a trefoil design in another colour, began to appear on many Victorian houses. Roof crests, usually of filigreed iron, also embellished the tops of roofs, often ornamented with Gothic crosses or fleurs-de-lys motifs. Even drainpipes, which were made of iron, had some Gothic emblem on them, as did rainwater heads, the more elaborate of which were shaped like a gargoyle or some other medieval figure.

In America, Downing wrote in *The Architecture of Country Houses* that the new pioneers required '[Picturesque] country houses with high roofs, steep gables, unsymmetrical and capricious forms. It is for

Gothic forms decorated gables, finials at the top of turrets and gables, and even roof ventilators. Pugin's designs for metalwork finials and ornamental gables were based on details taken from fifteenth- and sixteenth-century sources.

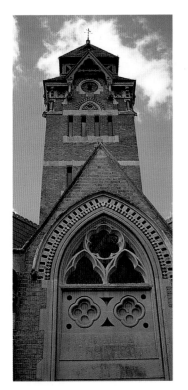

Asymmetrical, dominant rooflines were in stark contrast to the hidden roofs of the classical buildings which had been so popular at the start of the Victorian era. Tall, decorated brickwork chimney-stacks, deep sloping roofs topped with filigreed metalwork, richly carved gables – all added to the feeling of soaring verticality found on the exteriors of Gothic Revival houses.

[the man of imagination] ... that the architect may safely introduce the tower and the campanile – any and every feature that indicates originality, boldness, energy and variety in character.' However, as a footnote he added, 'excepting battlements – which have no meaning in the domestic architecture of this age'. His preferred exterior was the rural Gothic of Germany and England, with high ornamented gables wrought with tracery, bay windows and chimney-tops formed of moulded brick. He also suggested the addition of a Gothic-style cupola, which not only provided a feature 'very much to the good effect of the exterior' but was also practical, allowing outside ventilation – and thus 'pure air for the inmates of the house' – and disguising the external apparatus of 'unarchitectural and stove-pipe like' ventilation.

Gables – the triangular upper part of the wall between the sloping ends of a pitched roof – were important features on Gothic Revival houses, and they were usually richly carved and decorated. These were repeated above doorways and porches and over the tops of bay windows. Bargeboards, often in wood, at the peak of the gable were frequently to be found on American Gothic houses, and Downing wrote that these should be emphasised with sculptural ornament. His bargeboard designs were three-dimensional, with deep mouldings, and carved with pointed arches and crosses; these were later copied by rural carpenters, whose flatter, more 'naïve' wooden decorations became known in America as Carpenter Gothic style.

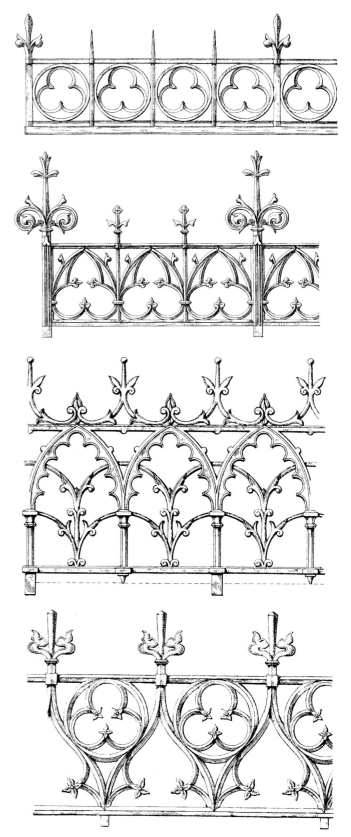

ABOVE: *Prominent chimney-stacks atop steeply pitched roofs adorned most Gothic Revival buildings. These* *designs for moulded brick-decorated chimneys were proposed by Downing for his rural Gothic villas.*

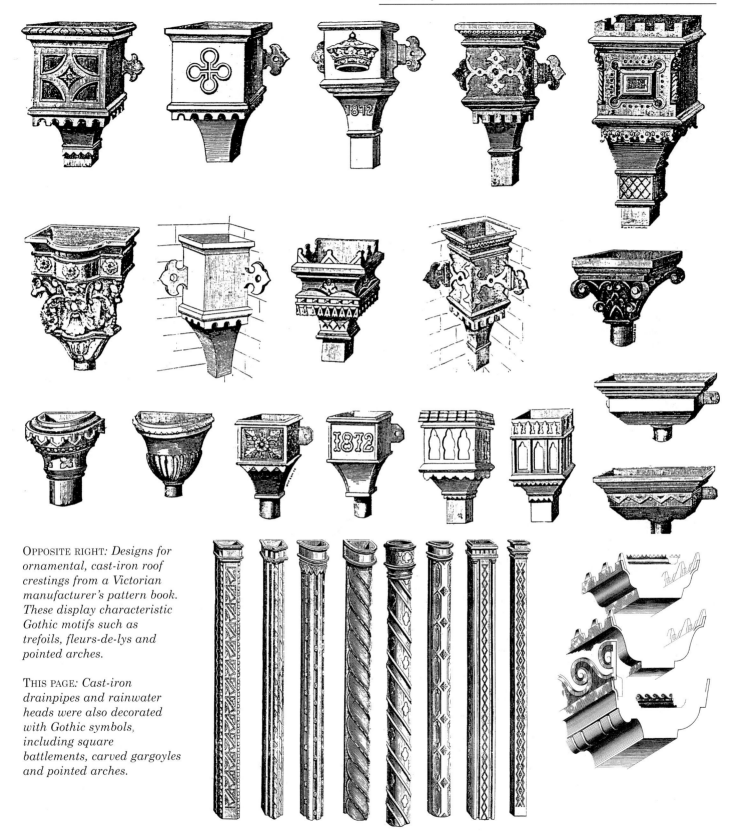

OPPOSITE RIGHT: *Designs for ornamental, cast-iron roof crestings from a Victorian manufacturer's pattern book. These display characteristic Gothic motifs such as trefoils, fleurs-de-lys and pointed arches.*

THIS PAGE: *Cast-iron drainpipes and rainwater heads were also decorated with Gothic symbols, including square battlements, carved gargoyles and pointed arches.*

Claremont House Inn

Rudloe Hall Hotel

Both in England and America, Gothic Revival homes rejected symmetry and, however simple, displayed a dazzling array of features on their façades.

One famous Carpenter Gothic house is 'The Wedding Cake House' in Kennebunkport, Maine. Remodelled in the 1850s by shipbuilder George Bourne, the original Federal house was ornamented with Gothic details, including wooden corner buttresses 'with panelled offsets and crocketed pinnacles terminating in turned finials high above the roofline'. The six buttresses resemble a medieval cathedral and support the cornices on the upper storeys, which are decorated with a petal pattern and capped by battlements. Other embellishments include Tudor-arched spandrels below the cornices, with quatrefoil and circle-patterned fretwork and pierced pendant skirtings, and one-storey-high subsidiary buttresses above the front entrance, which support a projecting cusped and crocketed trefoil-pierced ogee arch terminating in a poppyhead.

ABOVE: *The richly decorated exterior of 'The Wedding Cake House' – a fine example of American Carpenter Gothic style.*

BELOW: *Knightshayes in Devon, designed by William Burges in 1869. Eastlake wrote in* The Gothic Revival *that its 'massive walls, bold gables, stout mullions … are the principal incidents which give this building dignity and effect'.*

LEFT: *Eatington Park, a house built in 1858 by J. Prichard, which Eastlake described as embodying in its design 'much of those principles which were at one time identified with Mr Ruskin's name'.*

BELOW LEFT: *Porches were not just used as entrances but as meeting places for entire families and their guests. They often extended the entire width of the house as in the example illustrated here.*

BELOW: *The belfry of St Alban's Church, designed in 1858 by William Butterfield. It is decorated with polychromatic brickwork, for which Butterfield was famous.*

These houses from both sides of the Atlantic demonstrate the vast amount of variety possible – turrets, leaded lights, elaborate roof crestings, stained glass, porches and pointed windows – while still remaining within the style of Gothic Revival.

A selection of designs for Gothic houses which appeared in Edward Shaw's The Modern Architect *and Samuel Sloan's* The Model Architect, *two American manuals for housebuilders and carpenters that brought the Gothic style to a wider public and led to Gothic Revival homes being built across the length and breadth of the United States.*

Porches and Verandas

When Pugin was commissioned to remodel Scarisbrick Hall in 1837, his immediate solution for enlivening the façade of the garden side of the house was the addition of a porch with two canted turrets on either side of the door and a small, first-floor oriel window between them.

Elaborate porches displaying Gothic features often appeared at the entrances to Victorian Gothic villas and country houses, but they were also to be found on smaller suburban homes. Before the 1870s, when many terraced houses had basements, porches extended beyond the house, covering the bridge over 'the area'; once basements began to disappear, porches became part of the main building, adding an impressive entrance to even the simplest house, providing shelter from the rain, and making a feature of the recessed area leading to the front door, which was further embellished with decorative encaustic floor and wall tiles. These porches

OPPOSITE AND THIS PAGE: *In England, even modest Victorian houses and suburban villas had a decorative porch over the front door protecting the entrance from bad weather. These porches were primarily of wood or stone, carved with some form of Gothic motif. By contrast, in America verandas were attached to houses to shield the occupants from the sun and to provide an outside 'room' in which to sit.*

RIGHT: *The exteriors of many Victorian vicarages and small houses were given an ecclesiastical feel by their pointed-arch front doors and their railings.*

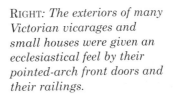

were constructed out of natural materials such as wood and stone, often carved with Gothic motifs, framed by pointed arches and topped with decorative gables.

Porch floors and walls were usually laid with geometrically patterned encaustic tiles (see pages142-3), but individual decoration also appeared and Burges even had a mosaic portrait of his pet dog in the front porch of the Tower House.

 Verandas, which are called 'porches' in America, were more common in the United States and Australia than in England because they provided an external living area during the long, hot summers. By protecting the exterior walls of a house from the sun, they kept the internal temperature down, while also giving the inhabitants somewhere cool and comfortable to sit outside. Furniture was wicker, often painted white or green, and the floors wooden, either painted to complement the colour of the house or covered with rush matting, a commodity newly arrived from East Asia. Additional colour and greenery were provided by hanging plants and jardinières.

As Downing wrote in connection with his design for a country house in the pointed, or Gothic, manner: 'In a cottage or villa of this style in England, the veranda would be useless, for the damp climate, so unlike ours, demands sun and air rather than shelter and shade.' One of his designs for a Gothic villa includes a broad, continuous veranda along the front of the house, with a large, central porch, pierced with arches on either side and opening on to the veranda, which projects 3.7 metres (12 feet) and breaks up 'the otherwise too long horizontal line of the veranda roof'. Veranda roofs were usually low-pitched or flat so as not to obscure the main building, and Downing emphasises the point that, as 'the spirit of the Gothic … style lies in the prevalence of vertical or upward lines', all long, unbroken lines should be avoided on the exteriors of this type of house.

Another of his designs for a Gothic villa has the veranda at the rear of the house, with the porch situated at the front entrance. An intricately carved bargeboard appears above the porch's gable, with a finial on top.

Railings and Gates
Railings and gates mark the boundary of a property. The growing numbers of middle-class property-owners in Victorian England were keen to make a statement about their status and wealth by delineating the borders of their houses.

Before the middle of the nineteenth century, most architectural ironwork was made of wrought iron, a metal that was malleable but very expensive to use. It was a very suitable material for intricate designs, especially for making copies of medieval metalwork, and Pugin developed a particular interest in reconstructing medieval patterns in wrought iron in conjunction with the Birmingham manufacturer,

John Hardman. However, most of Pugin's designs were for interior architectural fittings and smaller objects.

Mass-produced cast iron eventually superseded wrought iron, and designs for cast-iron gates and railings were soon being adapted from the hundreds of patterns in such books as L. N. Cottingham's *Smith and Founder's Director* (1824). Railings topped with Gothic crosses and fleurs-de-lys began to appear, as did gates with pointed arches, and builders' catalogues later in the century included a number of patterns suitable for Gothic houses.

Many detached Gothic houses, however, did not have railings around their boundary but were instead enclosed within a high brick wall; entry was through an arched wooden door or metal gate surrounded by carved stonework. The wall complemented the brickwork on the façade of the house and added an air of mystery to the house itself, which was not clearly visible from the street. On more modest terraced Gothic houses, the front boundary wall would be of brick, with a simple iron gate opening on to the path leading to the front door.

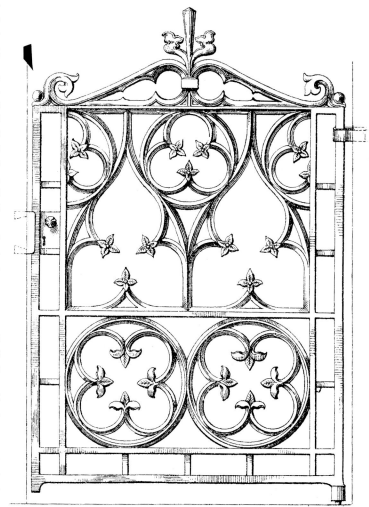

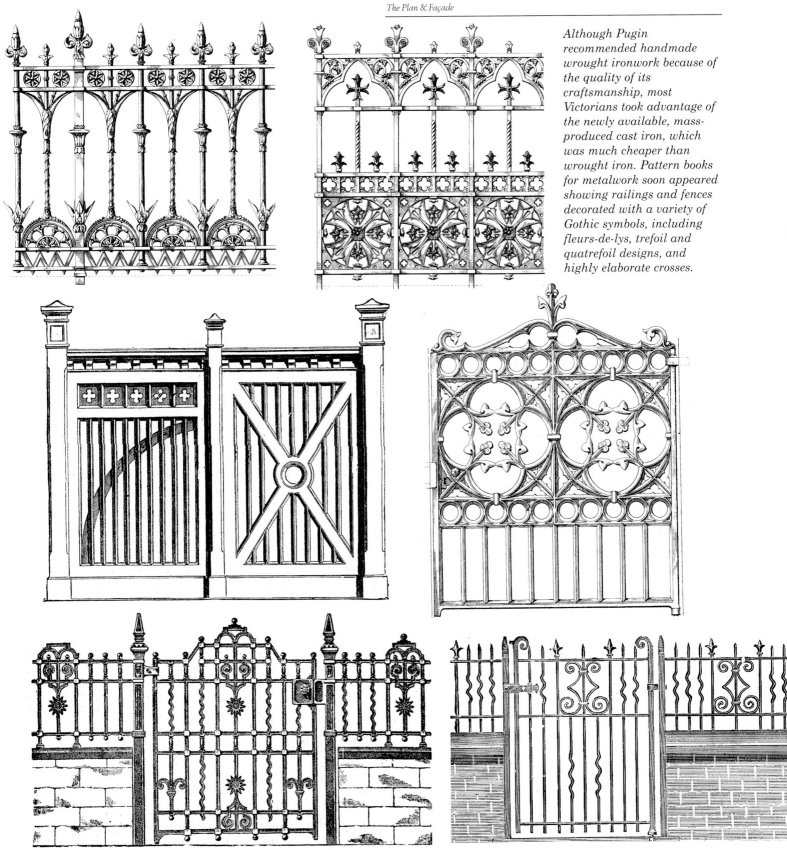

Although Pugin recommended handmade wrought ironwork because of the quality of its craftsmanship, most Victorians took advantage of the newly available, mass-produced cast iron, which was much cheaper than wrought iron. Pattern books for metalwork soon appeared showing railings and fences decorated with a variety of Gothic symbols, including fleurs-de-lys, trefoil and quatrefoil designs, and highly elaborate crosses.

For Victorians, an impressive front door made an important statement to the outside world, and therefore the front door of even a small house would have some form of decoration on it or framing it. On Gothic Revival houses, wooden doors with bold metalwork hinges and knockers, inspired by medieval examples, were typical features.

Doors

In Victorian England, where first impressions were important, the front door proclaimed to the visitor the social standing of the inhabitants of the house. An imposing front door was therefore an essential feature of the upper- and middle-class home.

On Gothic Revival houses, doors had to be specially made to fit the arched openings or the large entrances. The doors were primarily made of oak, with heavy strap hinges (elongated hinges resembling a leather strap), black iron bell-pulls, and brass or black iron knobs and knockers. Sometimes they were of solid wood with decorative arched panels, or they might have glazed panels within the door and a fanlight above, all filled with stained or painted glass. Larger Gothic villas and country houses usually had extremely grand front doors – Burges's Tower House even had a bronze one – with

highly ornamental metal or brass hinges and door furniture. Eastlake, in his *Hints on Household Taste*, deplored the use of cast iron on front doors and advised his readers that 'good wrought-iron knockers, of very fair design and manufacture, may be bought of the many medieval metal-workers whose branch of art has now become a recognised institution in this country'. Like other Gothic Revivalists, he believed that 'the work of the hammer and anvil is infinitely superior in every way to the production of the mould'.

As the use of natural materials was so important in the Gothic Revival movement, wooden doors were stained and varnished to protect them from the weather, not painted. However, on more modest Gothic houses where a cheaper wood like pine or deal was used, doors would either be grained or painted to prevent the knots in the wood from being exposed. Graining, an imitation

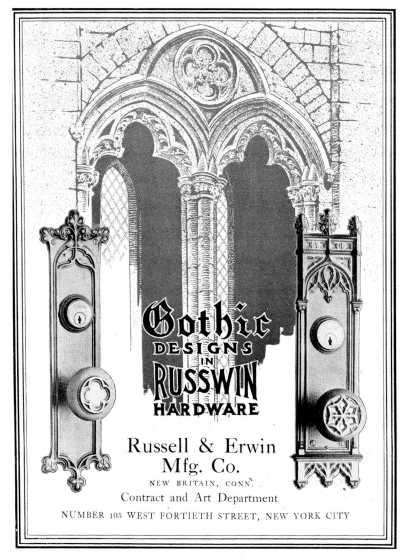

wood finish, was popular but had its critics, including Eastlake, who wrote that the practice was 'an objectionable and pretentious deceit, which cannot be excused even on the ground of economy'. If the front door was already painted, as often happened on a row of terraced houses where the housebuilder had painted it before the owner took possession, Eastlake advocated a 'good flat tint of olive green or chocolate colour'. This, he thought, would 'answer all practical purposes, and besides [is] more honest and artistic'. Dark blue was another fashionable colour, although brighter shades like red were also seen, especially later in the century.

Front doors were framed by carved stone, wood or brickwork arches, or set within a porch of timber, brick or stone. After the publication of Ruskin's books in the 1850s, front doors framed by columns with capitals of carved foliage also became a common feature.

Manufacturers' catalogues showing examples of doors and door furniture displaying the Gothic style became widely available during the second half of the nineteenth century. Pugin's source for his hinges and knockers (below centre) was the intricate metalwork found on the doors of medieval buildings and on furniture. He regarded such metalwork as 'rich and beautiful decorations' as well as being 'practically good'.

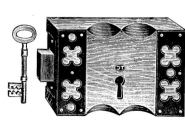

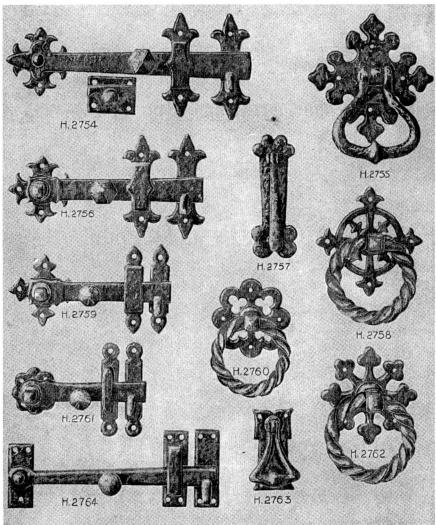

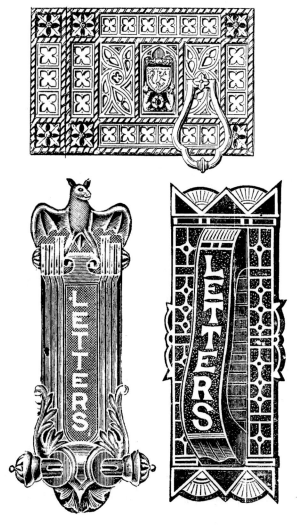

A distinguishing characteristic of Victorian Gothic houses is the wide variety of window treatments that can be found even on a single building. Oriels projecting from the first floor (top right and right) were originally a feature of medieval buildings, while Gothic arches, leaded window panes, tracery, gargoyles and floriated capitals all provide decorative interest to the façade of the house.

Windows

In the early nineteenth century, most houses tended to have symmetrically positioned, vertically sliding sash windows, with twelve panes of glass. However, the wider availability of sheet glass from 1838, and the abolition of window tax in 1851 and of the duty on glass in 1857, allowed windows to be made up of larger panes, and soon the six- and four-paned sash window predominated.

On Gothic Revival houses, however, a variety of windows were to be found. Grander houses often had large, square bay windows in their principal rooms, inset with tracery, leaded panes and stained glass. Pugin's first house, St Marie's Grange, had square-headed windows with mullions and uncusped lights. Square-headed windows often had wooden architraves in the shape of a Gothic arch and were Downing's preferred form of window for a Gothic villa; they also added, he felt, 'more domesticity' to a private house than the ecclesiastical-looking pointed arch.

Despite this, lancet windows with tall, narrow, pointed-arch tops, either on their own or set within tracery, were a common feature of Gothic Revival architecture, providing houses with a medieval look; casement windows with small panes and hinged vertically to the frame gave an appearance of cosiness, in contrast to the more elegant sash window; and oriel windows – which in medieval times were used as places of prayer – were frequently added to the façade of a house. The asymmetrical architecture of the Victorian Gothic house meant that a combination of these different types of windows could be incorporated into one building, adding interest to the façade as well as being appropriate to the function of the room where the window was sited.

However, plain sash windows were still used on many modest Victorian Gothic houses, but with pointed-arch stonework surrounds carved with trefoil and quatrefoil patterns. Lancet-shaped glass panes were also

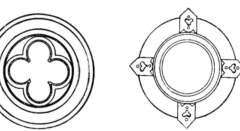
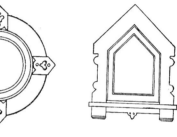

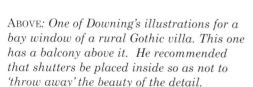

ABOVE: *One of Downing's illustrations for a bay window of a rural Gothic villa. This one has a balcony above it. He recommended that shutters be placed inside so as not to 'throw away' the beauty of the detail.*

RIGHT AND OPPOSITE BELOW LEFT: *Stained-glass panels inset with coloured glass 'to decorate front windows' were inspired by those found in medieval churches. These appeared in* Cassel's Household Guide.

sometimes inset into a square-framed sash window to provide a Gothic feature. Ruskin's well-known work, *The Stones of Venice,* influenced window design from the 1860s, and Venetian Gothic windows, with three lights grouped together – usually sashes with two small side lights and a large central one – and capped by a rounded Romanesque capital of carved foliage, soon appeared on many small Gothic villas and terraced houses.

Medieval-style features were also added to window surrounds in order to give a Gothic feel, including arched window hoods with carved wooden decoration, ornamental gables, bays with battlemented tops and square Tudor hood moulds.

Differences in climate between northern Europe and America also influenced the design of windows. As Downing wrote, in the Gothic villa abroad the 'window is made wholly to court the sunshine. Hence its exterior is ornamented with tracery, and made beautiful with carving'. In America, however, windows needed to be 'plain box-frames, with rising sashes and outside blind shutters, as the latter give us the power of regulating the light and coolness of our apartments in summer more perfectly than any other contrivance'. As outside shutters were necessary in order to protect interiors from extremes of temperature, Gothic tracery was not considered appropriate by Downing because the shutters 'would hide that which the architect labors to render attractive'.

As Gothic architecture was not a static style, restrained by strict rules, it could respond to the changing requirements of the environment and the individual. As Ruskin remarked about Gothic builders: 'If they wanted a window, they opened one; a buttress, they built one; utterly regardless of any established conventionalities of external appearance.' Victorian Gothic architects took this philosophy to heart, and the façades of their houses thus reflected the organic nature of this dynamic style.

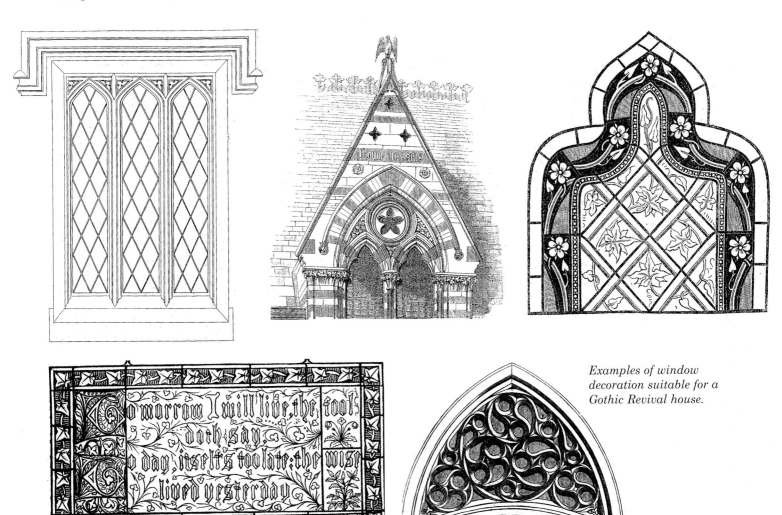

Examples of window decoration suitable for a Gothic Revival house.

Chapter 2
Halls, Stairs & Bedrooms

'As regards the hall, I have nailed my colours to the mast – a bay window, high open roof, lantern, two grand fire places, a great sideboard, screen, minstrel gallery – all or none.'

Pugin writing to the Earl of Shrewsbury about his design for the hall at Alton Towers

In an era where first impressions were all-important, the entrance hall in a Gothic Revival home – as in any style of Victorian house – had to impress visitors and proclaim the social status of the family within. This was easier to do in the large halls found in Gothic country houses and villas than in the narrow corridors of the Victorian terraced house. Nonetheless, the principle remained the same: as much attention was lavished on the décor of the entrance hall as on any other reception room in the house.

From as early as the 1820s, the grand hall began to reappear in larger houses as owners and architects hankered after the great halls of medieval and Elizabethan manor houses, romantically perceiving them to be the heart of the home. These great halls also inspired the Gothic Revival architects, who then proceeded to create richly decorated and imposing interiors for their wealthy patrons.

Such halls were not only seen as the entrance to the house but were also used as a banqueting hall or an additional reception room on festive occasions. Pugin particularly wanted to revive the medieval use of the great hall for social occasions. As he wrote in *True Principles*, the gentry in the Middle Ages 'did not confine their guests, as at present, to a few fashionables who condescended to pass away a few days occasionally in a country house; but under the oaken rafters of their capacious halls the lords of the manor used to assemble all their friends and tenants at those successive periods when the church bids all her children rejoice'. Scott declared in his *Remarks on Secular and Domestic Architecture* that halls also made 'a delightful sitting

Rudloe Hall Hotel

room', and later in the century, when halls began to be reduced in size, architects like Norman Shaw took up Scott's idea and designed them as an adjunct of the main living rooms.

The great halls normally rose to two storeys, with a gallery on the first floor. The walls were covered with dark wood panelling, usually of oak or mahogany, which was either in a linen-fold design, in the shape of Gothic arches, or richly carved with foliage, heraldic motifs, coats of arms or other symbols relevant to the owner of the house. The large bay or oriel windows had latticed panes, often inset with decorative stained glass, again displaying heraldry or coats of arms, and there would be an enormous fireplace to heat the room and ward off draughts. Ceilings were usually beamed – or ribbed – and, if space allowed, even vaulted to recreate a medieval atmosphere. Pugin's great hall at Scarisbrick had a spectacularly elaborate timbered ceiling decorated with stencilling and, as at Alton Towers, its own roof projecting above the skyline of the house.

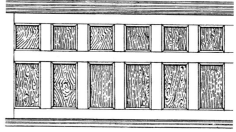

Even smaller Gothic villas and country houses had large entrance halls, which echoed the features of the baronial medieval hall. Many also had a vestibule or small porch between the front door and the entrance hall, which was entered by a tall, glass-panelled door. The vestibule doors, with their rich carving, beautiful stained-glass panes and heavy but intricately worked brass door furniture, marked the entrance into the house proper. These doors also served a practical purpose by shielding the main hall from draughts, and in winter they were hung with heavy, draped curtains, suspended on wooden or metalwork poles, to give additional protection from the cold.

Some later Gothic houses had colonnades of tall arches – either pointed or rounded – in the entrance hall framing the staircase and the doors into the main reception rooms. These arches rose from marble columns adorned with floriated capitals, which are evidence of the influence that Ruskin and his book, *The Stones of Venice*, had on interior design after the 1850s.

Wood panelling was the predominant feature of the Victorian Gothic hall. These examples range from a modest hall with simple panelling and banisters to a more impressive Reformed Gothic hall (above), as illustrated in Bruce Talbert's Gothic Forms Applied to Furniture, Metalwork and Decoration for Domestic Purposes.

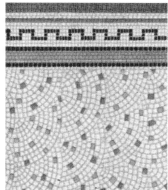

Mahogany or oak wainscoting (panelling), or softwood grained to look like it, were the preferred forms of wall decoration for larger halls, but real wood was too expensive for use in smaller homes. Instead, cheaper alternatives were slabs of paper stained and varnished to look like marble, which could easily be replaced if a section was damaged, or plaster scored while wet to resemble blocks of cut stone and then marbled. However, Eastlake condemned these as 'a sham', although 'a more excusable one', and advocated the use of inlaid encaustic tiles on the walls if real wainscoting could not be afforded. Tiles stretching 1-1.2 metres (3-4 feet) from the ground would, he felt, 'form an excellent lining for a hall or ground-floor passage', with paint or plaster washed with a 'flatted' colour above.

Flat-patterned geometric encaustic tiles were described by Eastlake as 'the best mode of treating a hall-floor'. In grander homes, more expensive inlaid mosaics were used instead.

RIGHT AND BELOW LEFT: *Heraldic shields and a hall table and mirror carved with Gothic decoration can give even a simple hallway a medieval feel.*

BELOW RIGHT: *Deep wood-panelled walls in the entrance hall and on the first-floor landing were a distinguishing feature of Gothic Revival houses.*

Wall colours depended on the amount of light entering the hall. If there was plenty of light coming in from large windows, then strong colours like Pompeian red were to be found; but in smaller houses, where the sole source of light might be from a fanlight above the front door, paler tones – a delicate green, warm grey or stone – were preferred.

Great halls would have a variety of objects hung on their walls, such as family portraits, tapestries, armour, antlers and coats of arms, while narrow hallways would have a simple mirror or a few small pictures framed in maple wood.

Hall floors were primarily inlaid with encaustic tiles, medieval or geometric patterns being the most popular. These floors were hard-wearing and easy to keep clean, and were often covered with oriental rugs or India matting. Some grander houses had specially designed

Arthur Brett & Sons Ltd

Deacon & Sandys

mosaic floors, and Burges's own home, Tower House, had a mosaic maze inlaid in its hall floor symbolising 'Time'. Terraced houses with narrow entrance halls would also have encaustic tiles on the floor, but with a runner or a narrow strip of dark green or brown oil-cloth on top.

Gothic Revival halls were usually furnished with specially created pieces that reflected the architecture of the room and which were also embellished with complementary medieval motifs. Furniture was usually of oak, giving the hall an appearance of solidity. In a large room there would be an imposing oak table flanked by chairs of the same wood, with hard seats that were not upholstered. These chairs often had pointed arched backs and other Gothic designs carved on them. Downing also recommended an antique settle made of oak or walnut as 'suitable for a large hall in the Gothic style'. Other pieces would include a hall stand for hats, cloaks and umbrellas, a grandfather clock, a carved oak 'ancestral' chest, a wooden bench, suits of armour, and

exotic flowers and foliage. The floral display could be set in wooden plant holders carved with arched panels, or even in a jardinière like the one exhibited at the Great Exhibition with its colour-printed Minton tile in a gilded brass frame.

If furniture was being bought and not individually made, Eastlake recommended that people look for 'ancient English' furniture because of its 'superior workmanship both as regards joinery and decorative carving'. As an example, in his *Hints on Household Taste* his illustration for a hall chair was taken from a Tudor manor house. For despite the rediscovery of traditional skills inspired by the Gothic Revivalists, Eastlake believed that most 'modern' furniture – or 'pseudo-Gothic joinery', as he called it – was of such poor quality that it 'becomes rickety in a few years, and rarely, if ever, survives a lifetime'.

Staircases and Landings

The staircase in a Gothic Revival house was an important feature of the entrance hall linking the ground and first floors, and it made an architectural statement as well. Staircase towers housing spiral staircases added to the asymmetrical structure of the building, often finished in a square tower or a steeply pitched roof with a finial or weathervane at the top. Light would filter into the stairwell via narrow lancet windows.

Pugin designed a staircase tower at the end of one wing of his house, St Marie's Grange, but he later found that an entrance staircase hall placed in a more central position provided a better plan and allowed more convenient circulation to the main rooms on the ground and first floors. The main staircase that he designed at Scarisbrick was fitted into a small rectangle, which was lit from above. With its 'spindly scaffolding', it was, as Mark Girouard observes in *The Victorian Country House*, Pugin's 'highly personal version of the continuous-newel staircases of the early seventeenth century'. At his later home, The Grange, he placed the entrance staircase hall in a tower with a lookout at the top. The staircase had a most unusual balustrade made from timber framing.

In a more traditional hall, the grand wooden staircase sweeping up to the first floor dominated the room. These large, open stairwells were designed to impress and were therefore seen as a rich source of decoration. Scott, in his *Remarks on Secular and Domestic Architecture,* advocated the Elizabethan style of staircase, with its 'bold, moulded string, carved, perhaps with running foliage, armorial bearings, mottoes, or inscriptions'. In staircases of 'a high degree of decoration', he also suggested the use of inlaid woods. Polished oak or mahogany side-panels were also embellished with other Gothic motifs, which echoed the rest of the hall or were in the shape of a medieval arch. In America, the sides of these staircases were also decorated with tiles or with painted or stencilled panels.

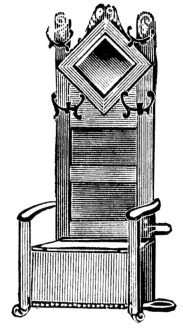

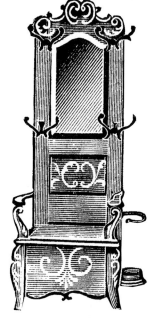

OPPOSITE AND THIS PAGE:
A selection of chairs and hat and cloak stands suitable for a Victorian Gothic hall. The old English carved chair (opposite) was illustrated by Eastlake as the perfect style for a hallway, while Downing recommended the antique settle (above left) made of oak or walnut, and with a leather cushion, for a 'large hall in a country house in the Gothic-style'.

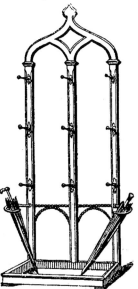

Balustrades were formed either of individual balusters from ornamentally turned wood in floral or Gothic shapes; or, as Scott wrote, of arcading, tracery or continuous scroll-work. Later in the century metalwork balusters began to appear, inspired by those used by Scott on the grand staircase at the Midland Hotel, built from 1868 to 1877. This staircase was designed in the Venetian Gothic style and was dramatically cantilevered on iron girders relief-cast with Gothic tracery. Handrails would usually be 'massive, to fit well to the hand', and of

Radloe Hall Hotel

Carved oak furniture and balustrading gave the entrance hall and staircase a feeling of seriousness and importance, conveying the respectability and economic status of the occupants. Today, craftsmen are reproducing furniture in the Reformed Gothic style (below right), combining medieval references with simpler forms of ornament, while some Gothic Revival homes display other styles of furniture (opposite left).

Paris Ceramics

Paris Ceramics

aTrevor Laurence

a smooth hardwood, such as mahogany, ending in a prominent newel post. The newel posts would often feature mythical animals, such as a griffin, or be surmounted by a decorative brass lamp or 'possibly, by figures or the supporters of the arms of the proprietor'.

Bizarre designs were not out of place on a Gothic Revival staircase, as can be seen on the baluster created by Burges for the staircase in the fifteenth-century octagon tower at Cardiff Castle: its top is in the shape of a crocodile, which to someone descending the stairs, seems to be looking at a baby crocodile on the rail beneath. At the bottom of the rail is a helmeted or muzzled lion, a figure symbolising the Bute family's royal connections.

Smaller terraced houses and villas had more modest staircases, placed at the end of the entrance hall, with a broader, curved bottom step to add importance. However, even ordinary staircases had carved balusters, which were either painted or of polished wood, with wooden handrails and newel posts.

Polished wooden stairs would either be left uncarpeted or have a central runner fixed with ornamental brass or iron carpet rods. On simpler stairs of a lesser-quality wood, the treads on either side of the runner would be painted in a rich shade of brown.

Unlike Victorian neo-Classical houses where the drawing room was on the first floor, and the main

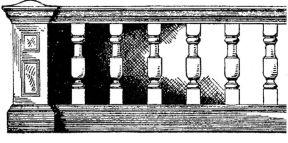

Wooden staircases dominated the entrance hall of even the smallest Gothic villa. Styles ranged from simple wooden ones with turned balusters, to highly ornate side-panels and banisters carved with scrollwork or in the shape of Gothic arches. From the 1870s, cast-iron staircases became popular, and intricately worked metal in the shape of crosses, fleurs-de-lys and quatrefoil designs (far right) complemented architectural and decorative Gothic features elsewhere in the house.

bedrooms on the upper floors, Gothic Revival homes normally had the reception rooms on the ground floor and the bedrooms on the first, with servants' quarters on an upper floor. Entrance hall staircases therefore led up to the bedrooms, which were reached either from the first-floor gallery off the main hall or from a large wood-panelled landing. Staircase towers usually opened into corridors or, as in Pugin's St Marie's Grange, on to rooms which opened out of one another. Large landing windows provided light, or, if this was a problem, an overhead skylight could be added, as Pugin did at Scarisbrick, to bring in light from above.

Rudloe Hall Hotel

Rudloe Hall Hotel

FAR LEFT AND ABOVE: *The staircase balusters of this Victorian Gothic mansion are of gilded metalwork. The staircase sweeps up to a landing lit by a huge stained-glass window, below which hangs a large tapestry, a form of wall decoration recommended by Pugin.*

LEFT: *Solid, polished wooden handrails were the most popular form for Victorian staircases.*

Langley Castle

LEFT AND FAR LEFT ABOVE: *Most large Victorian Gothic houses had an imposing stained-glass window on their landings and stairwells, often inset with the coats-of-arms of the inhabitants, or other heraldic symbols.*

FAR LEFT BELOW: *A timber-framed oak staircase at Langley Castle, a fourteenth-century battlemented tower house. Pugin's balustrading at The Grange was inspired by timber framing found in similar medieval buildings.*

BELOW: *Staircase runners were held in place with decorative cast-iron or brass stair rods.*

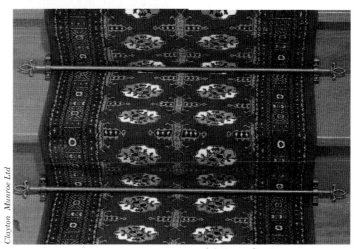

Clayton Munroe Ltd

Bedrooms

Unlike the main living rooms in a Victorian Gothic house, with their dark colours and carved wooden features, the bedroom was a place where light, warmth and simplicity predominated. Only in houses specially designed by the few leading Gothic Revival architects were there extravagant bedroom schemes, with medieval themes and motifs appearing on the interior decoration and the bedroom furniture.

Bedrooms became separate rooms only in the early years of the Victorian era when there was an increasing desire for privacy. In larger households, the husband and wife would each have their own bedroom, with an inter-connecting door; women might have, in addition, a private boudoir or sitting room; and same-sex children would share a bedroom, often on an upper storey where the nursery was to be found.

Hygiene was the primary concern in the bedroom as portable baths and chamberpots were used in them until later in the century when separate bathrooms began to appear. Bedrooms were also used as sickrooms and for giving birth in. Therefore, furniture, floors and fabrics had to be washed regularly and walls repainted in order to remove the dirt, dust and any bugs that had accumulated in the heavily draped bed furnishings and curtains and from the smoke of oil lamps and fires. Fireplaces were an important feature of the bedroom, not only for warmth but also for providing a through-draught, which ventilated the room and also helped to combat germs.

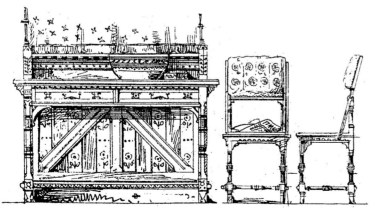

Style books told Victorians how to furnish their bedrooms in the appropriate fashion, an example of which is Talbert's illustrations for a suite of Gothic bedroom furniture (opposite). Eastlake, in his Hints on Household Taste, *recommended an iron bedstead with canopy (above),* while Henry Shaw's Specimens of Ancient Furniture *(1836) showed a heavily carved four-poster bed (right). Downing, in* The Architecture of Country Houses, *proposed this interior (above right) for an upper storey bedroom in a Gothic country house.*

Guild of Master Woodcarvers

Guild of Master Woodcarvers

Guild of Master Woodcarvers

As bedrooms were private areas, and therefore unseen by most visitors, their decoration and furniture were much simpler than those found in the more public rooms of the house. Ceilings were primarily flat, with a simple Gothic cornice of a trefoil, quatrefoil or floral pattern, although upper-storey bedrooms could reflect a Gothic style by having a high ribbed ceiling with exposed rafters. These would be stained and varnished, and the space in between plastered. As Downing noted, 'This gives a lofty bed-room, combining spaciousness and good effect with a fine circulation of air.'

Gothic Revival architects designed bedrooms in rich, sombre tones, as can be seen in Pugin's State Bedroom and Lord Chancellor's Bedroom at the Palace of Westminster with their linen-fold oak panelling on the walls and, respectively, their deep red and green wallpaper in a single flock pattern above. The bedroom that Burges created for the Marquis of Bute at Cardiff

Rudloe Hall Hotel

ABOVE: *Carved oak beds were the predominant feature of the Victorian Gothic bedroom, with their rich decoration displaying Gothic motifs and their elaborately turned posts echoing those found in medieval times.*

LEFT AND OPPOSITE: *Unlike the heavily draped hangings found on many Victorian beds, Victorian Gothic drapery was much simpler in style. The canopy over the bedhead at Langley Castle has taken its inspiration from medieval references.*

Castle had reddish-brown woodwork on the walls, but with a gilded ceiling painted and inset with mirrors, while the colours he chose for Lady Bute's bedroom at Castell Coch at the top of a round tower were dull gold, green and red.

While these strong colours were used in individually commissioned bedrooms – and are appropriate for interior decoration today when recreating a Victorian bedroom in a Gothic Revival house – most Victorians themselves felt that the bedroom, whatever the style of house, should be painted in soft, feminine shades of seashell pink, pale green or pearly grey. One anonymous writer in *The Workwoman's Guide* (1838) even listed a range of possible colours suitable for a bedroom: 'Blue is pretty, but rather cold; yellow gives great cheerfulness, as also pink, but the latter is apt to fade too soon and is perhaps a little too shewy. Crimson, claret, stone-colour, buff, and light green all look well; a darker green is very refreshing to the eye, and therefore suitable for very light sunny rooms.' Painted walls were preferred to wallpaper because they could be washed down and repainted regularly for hygienic reasons (wallpaper was believed to harbour insects such as bed bugs), although later in the century, when thinner and less expensive wallpapers were being mass-produced and general standards of cleanliness had improved, printed patterns of flowers and fruit began to appear on bedroom walls.

Fitted wall-to-wall carpets were discouraged in the bedroom because they could not be taken up and beaten regularly. Floors were therefore of wood, which was stained or oiled and then varnished, and covered with oriental or rag rugs or rush matting, so that they could be swept and cleaned easily. More modest bedrooms and nurseries had linoleum or cork matting on their floors.

Curtains tended to echo the décor of the bedroom. In wealthier homes, velvets, satins and antique brocades would be used on the windows and bed furnishings, while simpler bedrooms would have drapery made from lighter chintzes, lace or muslin, which not only let light into the room but also allowed fresh air to circulate. In America it was common to add a transparent layer of muslin or lace – or more expensive silk or satin – over either the whole window or just the lower half, which was supposed to soften any 'glare' from outside. Wooden shutters or simple muslin blinds were also found on bedroom windows, especially where there were narrow lancet windows in the room.

Bedroom furniture

Eastlake summed up the Victorians' love of filling the bedroom with furniture, heavily curtained beds and windows, and lace-covered dressing tables overflowing with decorative trinkets, writing: 'As a rule, our modern bed-rooms are too fussy in their fitting up. A room intended for repose ought to contain nothing which can fatigue the eye by complexity.'

The most important item of furniture was obviously the bed, which at the start of the Victorian era was a four-poster made out of mahogany or beechwood, with its head- and footboards joined together by iron side-bars, and with full curtains around it for privacy. However, because these heavy drapes harboured germs, wooden half-testers soon became more popular with their canopy extending a little over a metre (about 3 feet 6 inches)

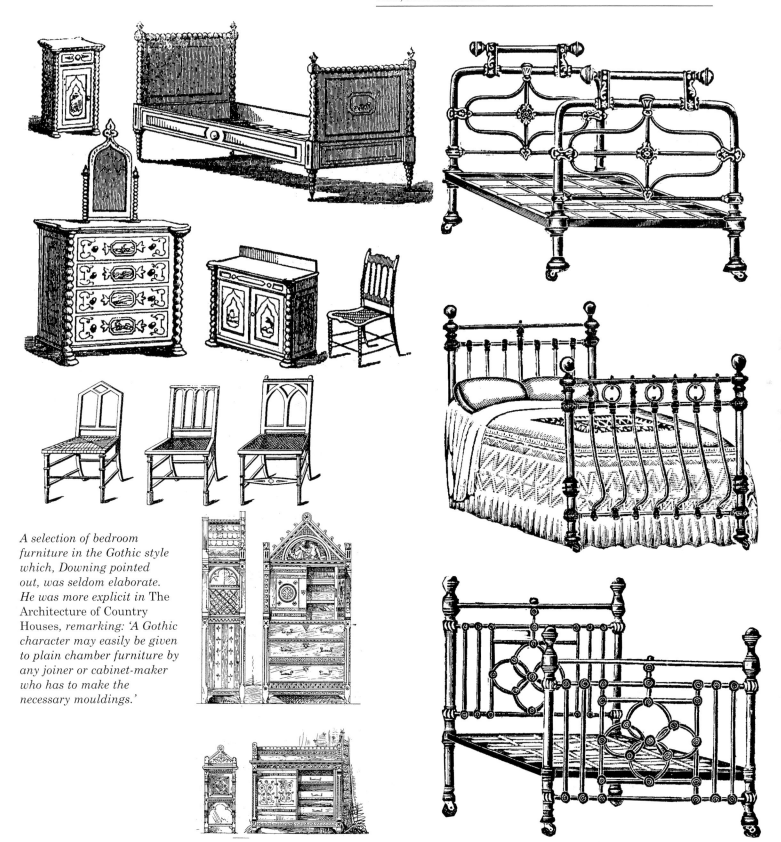

A selection of bedroom furniture in the Gothic style which, Downing pointed out, was seldom elaborate. He was more explicit in The Architecture of Country Houses, *remarking: 'A Gothic character may easily be given to plain chamber furniture by any joiner or cabinet-maker who has to make the necessary mouldings.'*

over the headboard and with simple side curtains tied back when not in use. By the 1860s iron and brass bedsteads with no drapery at all were viewed as the most hygienic way to sleep.

The heavily carved wooden beds preferred by the Gothic Revivalists, so reminiscent of those used in the Middle Ages, had elaborately turned posts and decorative carving in the form of Gothic motifs, arched panels and tracery both on their head- and footboards and at the top of their canopies. Some of these headboards were also inset with painted panels, like the scene from Tennyson's poem *'The Day Dream'* on

Deptich Designs

Deptich Designs

ABOVE AND ABOVE RIGHT: *Heavy drapery began to lose popularity as the century progressed and brass beds came to be considered the healthy alternative.*

Shortland

Shortland

Shortland

Langley Castle

ABOVE AND OPPOSITE BELOW: *Pointed arches on panels of cupboard doors and framing alcoves contribute significantly to a Victorian Gothic atmosphere in a modern bedroom, as would an iron bed with matching chair and bedside table displaying typical Gothic motifs.*

LEFT: *Medieval-style bedhangings in a bedroom at Langley Castle complement the original fourteenth-century architecture of the room.*

Burges's own bedhead at the Tower House. Later, when brass and iron beds became fashionable, they were also forged into Gothic shapes.

Today, a medieval style can be recreated in the bedroom with either an original four-poster wooden bed, such as can still be found in antique shops, or one of the good reproductions now being made. A more modern interpretation, however, would be to omit the full drapery around the bed and allow the beauty of the carving to stand out. The dark, heavy frame can then be given an air of lightness by the addition of crisp white bedlinen and lace-covered pillows.

The next most important piece of furniture was the wardrobe, which was usually double-fronted with a central bevelled mirror. Elaborate Gothic bedroom furniture was rare, but Downing wrote that a plain wardrobe with Gothic arched panels could easily be made from 'handsome black-walnut' with a panel filled with 'a single plate of looking-glass'. Such a basic design, he felt, would be 'at once chaste and rich enough for any country house'. Built-in wardrobes did not become fashionable until the 1880s, but wall-to-wall cupboards in today's home can be made to reflect a Gothic style by the simple addition of pointed-arched panels to their fronts and doors.

Other furniture and decorative items in the bedroom included a cheval mirror; dressing tables covered with a variety of bric-à-brac such as silver-topped perfume bottles, ivory, tortoise-shell or silver brushes, combs and hand mirrors, candlesticks and ring-holders; marble-topped washstands with decorative bowls and jugs, even after the introduction of separate bathrooms; a wooden towel-horse nearby; a few light bedroom chairs and possibly a 'fainting' couch at the foot of the bed. Carved wooden chests with intricate metal ironmongery, inspired by medieval sources, were also found in Gothic Revival bedrooms placed either at the end of the bed or along a wall, and these provided additional storage for bed-linen and other items. Other specialist pieces were cabinets and display stands, painted, carved and gilded with medieval imagery and motifs. In Burges's guest bedroom at the Tower House, for example, there was a painted 'Philosophy Cabinet' illustrating the personal problems that can intrude into the lofty thoughts of philosophers, while in his own bedroom a giltwood stand held some of the caskets from his large collection.

THIS PAGE AND OPPOSITE: *Decorated jugs and wash-basins were a standard feature in any Victorian bedroom, even after the introduction of separate bathrooms, as were silver-topped scent bottles.*

SILVER-MOUNTED TOILET REQUISITES—contd.

Silver-mounted Scent Bottles, with Silver Shoulders

No. 3287. Size 4¾ in. high 31/0
" 3286. " 4¼ " " 26/0
" 3285. " 3¾ " " 19/6

Plain Silver Scent Flask.

No. 834.
Size 3¼ by 1⅞ in.   7/6

Silver-mounted Scent Bottles.

No. 3248.
Cherub.
5⅛ by 3¼ in.
21/0

No. 3247.
Hammered.
4½ by 3⅛ in.
17/0

No. 3246.
Plain.
4¼ by 2½ in.
14/0

Silver-mounted Scent Bottles.

No. 782/2.   In case 50/0

Scent Flask.

No. 888.
[Size 2⅜ by 1⅝   5/0

Silver-mounted Scent Bottle.

No. 13224.
Size 3 in.................. 17/6
"   3½ in.............. 22/0

Scent Flask.

No. 878.
Size 3⅛ by 1¼.
6/0

Silver-mounted Scent Bottles, in case.

No. 775/7423.   Bottles, size 3 in.
Pierced silver shoulders 28/0

No. 2242.
Bottles, 5¼ in. high, in case 67/6

Silver-mounted Scent Bottles.

No. 3063.
Size 5 by 4 in. 21/0

No. 3064.
4½ by 3½ in. 16/6

No. 3065.
3⅝ by 3 in. 13/0

No. 3257.
Cherub.
5½ by 2½ in. 21/0

No. 3252.
Plain.
5⅛ by 2⅛ in. 17/0

Silver-mounted Scent Bottles, in Cases.   No. 834.

Silver-mounted Bottles in Cases.

No. 3172.

2 bottles in pigskin case, size 4¼ in.... 16/0

2 do. do. in crocodile case 20/0

3 do. do. in pigskin case, size 4¼ in.... 23/0

3 do. do. in crocodile case 28/0

Silver-mounted Lavender Salts Jars.

No. 4636.

No. 4636.
Hammered mount, size 3½ in. 11/0
Plain mount, size 2¾ in.   7/0
Chased mount, size 2½ in. 6/0

No. 834.
In leather case, lined satin, containing 2 silver-mounted bottles 22/0

Chapter 3
Living Rooms

'A great beauty of this style, when properly treated, is the home-like expression which it is capable of, in the hands of a person of taste. This arises, mainly, from the chaste and quiet colours of the dark wood-work, the grave, though rich hue of the carpets, walls, etc., and the essentially fireside character which the apartments receive from this kind of treatment....The prevailing character [of the Gothic is] of the quiet domestic feeling of the library and the family circle.'

A.J. Downing, The Architecture of Country Houses

OPPOSITE: *A simple refectory table, chair backs with arched panels, a large, central metalwork chandelier and an oriental rug; these convey the feeling of a Victorian Gothic dining room in a modern setting.*

Whatever the architectural style of the Victorian home, the main living rooms included a drawing room, a dining room, and a morning room or parlour. Larger houses also had a library, a billiards room and a smoking room.

These reception rooms were the public rooms of the house and were therefore situated in the best position on the main floor, and decorated and furnished more lavishly than elsewhere. Entertaining took place in the drawing room and dining room, while more private family life was conducted in the morning room or parlour. Some houses had a front and back parlour separated by heavy sliding doors, the front being a place in which to receive visitors while the back acted as a library and a music room as well.

Although the prevailing feeling of the Gothic house was masculine, with its dark woodwork on the walls and floors, and deep, rich interior decoration – a style well suited to dining rooms and libraries – the drawing room and parlour were more feminine in tone because these areas were where the women in the household spent their time in domestic and creative pursuits. As Robert Kerr wrote in his influential book, *The Gentleman's House* (1864), 'The character to be always aimed at in the drawing room is especial cheerfulness, refinement of elegance, and what is called lightness as opposed to massiveness ... the rule in everything is this ... to be entirely ladylike.'

Many Victorian Gothic homes adopted exaggerated medieval features in their living-room décor and furnishings, a style criticised by Pugin as unsuitable for domestic interiors. As he complained in *True Principles*, 'Everything is crocketed with angular projections,

Rudloe Hall Hotel

ABOVE: *The valance to the curtains in the drawing room of this renovated Victorian Gothic mansion emulates a similar window treatment that was sketched by Andrew Jackson Downing in his work* The Architecture of Country Houses.

Light Innovation

BELOW: *A detail from a dining room in a Tudor house in Devon, which Eastlake recommended in* Hints on Household Taste *as a good example of the Old English style.*

innumerable mitres, sharp ornaments, and turreted extremities. A man who spends any length of time in a modern room, and escapes without being wounded by some of its minutiae, may consider himself extremely fortunate.' For Pugin, embellishing the essential construction of a room or of pieces of furniture was acceptable; whereas introducing pinnacles, groining, tracery, and so on, as mere decoration was 'contrary to the spirit of the style, which does not admit of the introduction of these features in any situation but that to which they properly belong'.

Floors were normally of wood with flat-patterned carpets laid on top, but with a 60-centimetre-(2-foot-) wide margin left around the perimeter of the room (see page 137). Wealthier homes that could afford more expensive woods had polished, patterned parquetry on their drawing-room and library floors covered with a variety of oriental rugs.

Curtains and upholstery in Gothic living rooms were also much simpler than the fussy, overblown drapery found in other styles of Victorian décor, with the emphasis on richness of fabric and textile design rather than on frills and ornate, decorative treatments (see pages 135-9).

The Drawing Room and Parlour

Gothic Revival houses may have had internal Gothic architectural features, but many had interiors and

OPPOSITE RIGHT: *Pugin's illustration in* True Principles *showing an 'extravagant style of Modern Gothic Furniture and Decoration', an interior 'covered with trifling details' which, he believed, was 'subversive of good effect'.*

LEFT: *Talbert's illustration of a drawing room decorated and furnished in the Reformed Gothic style.*

BELOW: *A drawing of 'The Conditions of Life' escritoire designed by Burges and painted by C. Rossiter, with a Moorish-style chair beside it, published in* Building News *in 1874.*

furnishings reflecting an amalgam of decorative styles. Although some drawing rooms had no dado and were painted in pale colours – including cream, lavender, pearl grey and blue – surrounded by gilt moulding, as favoured by other styles, panelled woodwork was the dominant feature of Gothic interior walls. The panels were carved with linen-fold patterns, Gothic arches and heraldic motifs, although by the 1860s simpler, more geometric Gothic forms began to appear.

Deep friezes, sometimes painted or carved, decorated the top of the wall, while the area in between was painted or hung with flat-patterned wallpapers (see pages 129-35) inspired by Pugin's designs. By the 1850s, however, decorative schemes favoured darker, stronger colours such as sage green, Prussian blue, indigo, gold and rusty reds.

The early Gothic Revivalists also hung antique textiles and tapestries on their walls. Then in the 1860s and 1870s, Reformed Gothic designers advocated replacing wallpaper with patterned wool or embroidered wall hangings that were handmade by the new generation of craftsmen. Paintings were also suspended from a decorative brass rail that would run round the room below the frieze.

A large fireplace – 'the sacred family altar' – with a chimneypiece highly decorated with Gothic motifs dominated the room (see pages 144-9).

Furniture was arranged asymmetrically around the room in conversational groupings, and even Gothic

LEFT: *Large, square bay windows of stained glass, often inset with heraldic shields, were a common feature of the Victorian Gothic drawing room.*

OPPOSITE: *A simple window treatment enhances the fine Gothic window of this grand drawing room. The curtains are held back with decorative pins during the daytime.*

Langley Castle

Revivalists adopted the Victorian tendency to cram the drawing room with furniture, although furnishings and furniture designs were much simpler than other decorative styles. As Hermann Muthesius wrote in his *Das Englische Haus* published in 1904 – although what he said is equally applicable to the Victorians half a century earlier – the aim was to make the drawing room 'the jewel casket of the home, in both content and form ... in many houses it has almost become a museum of old, valuable furniture and art treasures, and is often filled to overflowing in the process'.

Drawing-room furniture might include a sofa, a central table, some comfortable upholstered chairs as well as an assortment of other small chairs and side tables for writing, cards and chess, an étagère – a large, tiered piece placed against a wall to display ornaments, which was especially popular in America – footstools, wall cabinets, screens and even a grand piano. Although the well-known Victorian Gothic architects designed individual pieces of furniture for their domestic commissions, these were not widely available and, as Downing pointed out, 'Well-designed furniture in this style is rarely seen in this country [America], and is far from common on the other side of the Atlantic'.

Pugin's furniture designs, which he conceived as integral parts of his overall schemes, were made up for him from the 1840s by J. G. Crace, John Webb and G. Myers, as well as Gillow and Holland, and took their inspiration from Tudor and Jacobean sources rather than continuing the fussy perpendicular lines found on his early pieces. Downing and Eastlake also favoured Elizabethan or Flemish styles because they combined 'the picturesque and the domestic' more successfully than Gothic furniture. Ecclesiastical-looking chairs were considered by Downing as 'too elaborate' for most private houses, and instead he recommended achieving the appropriate effect by covering simple Gothic furniture 'with rich stuffs' rather than with 'elaborate Gothic carving', which, he believed, was 'usually rather severe and angular, when applied to furniture'.

OPPOSITE ABOVE*: Downing's interior for a parlour in a simple Gothic style, with a Tudor arched bay window at one end and a square-headed window with an arch in the woodwork of the architrave on the side.*

OPPOSITE BELOW*: An inglenook fireplace at Farnham Park, designed by Richard Norman Shaw. Eastlake in* The Gothic Revival *commented how 'picturesque and interesting an object a fireplace may become when designed by an artist's hand'.*

LEFT*: The interior of The Limes in Dulwich, designed by architect Theodore Howard in 1881. In this house, Howard, whose family firm manufactured neo-Puginesque furniture, intentionally linked the Gothic Revival with the Aesthetic movement.*

BELOW LEFT*: A drawing-room commode by Charles Bevan, a Reformed Gothic furniture designer, which was illustrated in* House Furnisher *in 1871.*

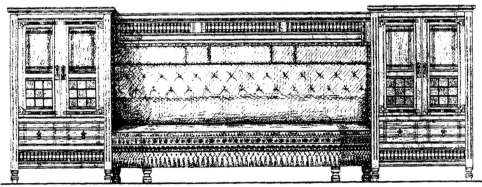

Thistle Joinery Ltd

Gothic arches, gables and fleur-de-lys finials give a medieval appearance to modern bookshelves in a drawing room.

Eastlake wrote that 'the best and most picturesque furniture of all ages has been simple in general form ... its main outlay [being] always chaste and sober in design, never running into extravagant contour or unnecessary curves'. A seventeenth-century sofa found at Knole was, for him, an ideal style for a drawing room, while the proportions of a typical Elizabethan chair, with its low seat and high padded back, which was 'strange' to the Victorian eye, could be adapted to modern usage by substituting 'a few incised patterns

Wooden cabinets and sideboards, carved with Gothic details and often finished with bold metalwork, were amongst the many pieces of furniture found in the Victorian living room. Decoratively worked brass lamps and candlesticks provided the lighting.

and turned mouldings' for 'the lumpy carving and "shaped" legs usually found in such furniture'. These simple oak constructions should then be covered with velvet and trimmed with silk fringing.

The Reformed Gothic furniture designs of Norman Shaw and Bruce Talbert were bolder and more primitive than Pugin's; however, even though they were stripped of ornament, their Gothic forms still maintained a general reference to medievalism, and their repeating geometric patterns, intricate metalwork with wrought-brass hinges, and polychromatic decoration were a great source of inspiration to later Arts and Crafts designers.

A selection of drawing-room furniture and musical instruments in the Reformed Gothic style. OPPOSITE, CLOCKWISE FROM TOP LEFT: *A medieval cabinet organ designed by Charles Bevan in 1866; one of Talbert's drawing-room interiors; a medieval-style piano by Bevan, 1866; and a sideboard illustrated in* Hints on Household Taste.

THIS PAGE: *Downing suggested the highly carved chairs (left) for a typical Gothic drawing room, and showed the drawing room at Kenwood, near New York (below left), as an example of how a whole room should look. Eastlake believed the seventeenth-century chairs (below) and sofa (bottom left) were the ideal forms of seating for the drawing room.*

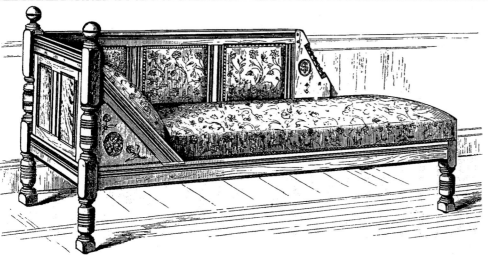

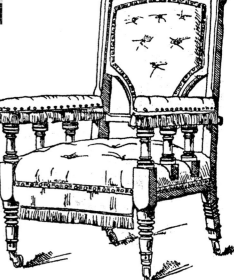

Mark Wilkinson

Trevor Lawrence

Cohen & Pearce

The Dining Room

Loudon believed that 'the characteristic colouring of a dining room should be warm, rich and substantial', while Kerr in *The Gentleman's House* wrote that the décor should be 'somewhat massive and simple', with the overall appearance of the room being 'of masculine importance'. The dining room was, after all, a male preserve where men remained to talk and smoke after dinner when the women had 'retired', and this air of masculinity was ideally suited to Victorian Gothic decoration. Its welcoming tones and materials not only conveyed an air of hospitality but looked attractive by candlelight, the most popular form of lighting at the dinner table – although chandeliers and wall sconces also lit the room.

Wood panelling which either covered the wall or went up to dado level was also a feature that was both

OPPOSITE AND THIS PAGE:
The masculine feel of the Victorian dining room was emphasised by the dark, wood-panelled walls and the solid wooden furniture, which in Gothic homes echoed some of the architectural details of the room. A galleried area in a dining room added a medieval touch to the room by giving it the appearance of a banqueting hall with a minstrels' gallery.

consistent with the style and practical, protecting walls from being damaged by chair backs. Until the late 1860s, dining-room chairs were not placed around the table but lined up along the wall. The rest of the wall up to the carved, moulded cornice was covered with a dark-coloured flock paper – for example, crimson or deep green – over which imposing family portraits were suspended from gleaming brass picture rails.

A large fireplace and chimneypiece – in some cases echoing that of a medieval banqueting hall – together with a brass or wrought-iron grate and firedogs completed the interior.

Overall, James Arrowsmith in his *The Paper Hanger's and Upholsterer's Guide* (1854) recommended 'Few ornaments [in the dining room] … beyond the display on the sideboard, the walls coloured in distemper, or painted flat in oil of a warm colour, with gold or japanned mouldings; panelling in imitation of oak is also appropriate; the curtains claret or crimson cloth, trimmed with gold coloured orris lace, a brass rod with a plum fringed valance, or a valance alone are sufficiently genteel … A turkey carpet is most suitable, and from its durability, economical, but Axminster or Brussels in suitable colours are very good substitutes.'

The room was furnished with a (usually mahogany) dining-room table at its centre, a matching set of six or twelve chairs, and a large sideboard displaying the

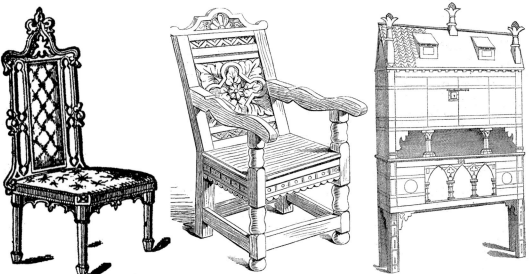

The sideboard, or cabinet, was an important piece of furniture in the dining room. Talbert's design (above) was exhibited at the Royal Academy in 1870, while Burges's painted cabinet (left) was criticised by Christopher Dresser in the Technical Educator: *'The windows together with the tiled roof degrade the work to a mere doll's house in appearance.'* Dining-room chairs were ranged around the walls of the room and not around the table.

OPPOSITE: *In smaller homes – as in today's houses – where space was limited, the library formed part of the dining room.*

LEFT: *The dining room in one of the Gothic Revival houses at Holly Village, north London.*

BELOW: *Victorian dining-room tables were less elegant than those of earlier periods, with Gothic-style tables being plainer and more structural in form than other, heavier Victorian styles.*

family's best silver and porcelain. Pugin designed a range of dining-room chairs for his interiors, including one with an X-frame and another with barley-sugar twist legs and a square, padded leather back and seat, which he later adapted for the Houses of Parliament by gothicising the legs. Other chairs were inspired by early Spanish and Flemish designs.

As for Pugin's tables, initially they were 'modern' shapes but with gothicised forms. However, by the 1840s the shapes were more architectural – for example, a plain refectory table and a simple octagonal table – and these furniture designs were characterised by the use of revealed tenons ('the projecting end of a piece of wood formed to fit into a corresponding mortise in another piece') and chamfering ('the cutting of a plane on the diagonal, across a right angle, to create a polygonal silhouette'). These structural forms also inspired later Reformed Gothic and Arts and Crafts designers, and Pugin's influence was clearly visible in their work. Eastlake also illustrated a number of suitable styles of dining-room table, and recommended one dating from the Jacobean period as being 'of a very simple but picturesque design, and is certainly sound in principle of construction'.

Sideboards were an important piece of dining-room furniture and were ripe for the varying types of embellishment loved by the Gothic Revivalists. Examples of two imaginatively decorated sideboards are the one displayed by Burges at the 1862 London Exhibition, which E. J. Poynter painted to Burges's

Arthur Brett & Son Ltd

Trevor Laurence

design of 'The Battle between the Wines and the Spirits', with four cameos representing Ginger Beer, Lemonade, Seltzer Water and Soda Water inside its doors; and furniture designer J. P. Seddon's inlaid oak sideboard, whose style *Building News* described in 1865 as 'founded on Early Geometrical Gothic, but treated completely in subordination to practical requirements, to which no other style lends itself so readily'. Its decorative details included an arcade of small columns, red-and-green enamelled hinges, a mirror supported on pilasters with a roof on top, and a leather panel underneath the plate rack painted with stylised flowers.

Sideboards were ripe for decoration. They displayed a variety of extravagant detail and allowed the family to show off its collection of china, metalwork treasures and other ornaments. The tables (opposite below right) are two of Eastlake's suggested styles for the Gothic dining room.

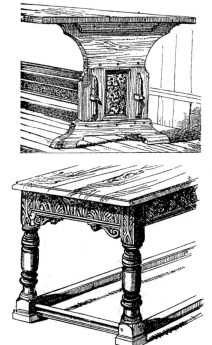

Trevor Laurence

The Gothic style was ideally suited to the book-lined library, where seriousness and scholarship was the atmosphere to be achieved. Today, most houses do not have the space for a separate library; nevertheless, copies of original bookcases, carved with Gothic arches and other medieval details, and placed within a modern living room, readily recreate this feeling of learning.

The Library

As Loudon wrote in 1838, 'in the present day, no villa, or suburban residence, having more than two sitting-rooms, can be considered complete without a library'. A library was not only a room to house books, but was the equivalent of a morning room for men, and most middle-class homes aspired to have one.

Libraries were viewed as a Gothic sanctuary for most of the nineteenth century, with their oak-panelled bookcases, leather-upholstered seating, wonderful array of books with rich leather bindings and a lectern on which to display some precious manuscript. The room would also house a desk and a central library table with a leather top (Eastlake recommended dark green as being 'best suited to oak'). The mood conveyed by this style of décor was scholarly, and according to Downing, 'quiet and grave in manner'.

Pugin's design for the library at Taymouth Castle c.1837 was described as being 'fitted up in the richest Gothic style' and having the effect of 'a grand Gothic

Tower of past centuries. The under tier windows and all the details of the Building are taken from an old castle in Normandy.'

At Tyntesfield in Somerset, which was remodelled in the 1860s by architect John Norton, who had studied under one of Pugin's pupils, the great library was lined with oak shelves, oak-panelled walls and an open oak roof. As Girouard writes, 'The warm brown of books and woodwork set off the richer colouring of the Chinese and Japanese porcelain on the gable wall and above the bookcases; at one end an archway opens onto a huge bay window ... the result is one of the most liveable and sympathetic of Victorian libraries.'

Bookcases reflected the architecture of the room. Gothic styles included gables, traceried glass fronts and pointed-arch details framing shelves and on door panels.

Downing's preference for bookcases in a Gothic villa was based on two 'very correct and satisfactory' designs by Loudon: 'When there is a large collection of books to be provided for, either of these designs may be adopted, and extended along both sides or all round the library.'

Eastlake called for bookcases and library doors to be made of solid oak, with the mouldings worked in it, as opposed to being applied to it, as best for 'both appearance and durability'. Mahogany was an alternative wood, 'which acquires a good colour with age', and which could also be 'stained black and covered with a thin varnish'. If expensive woods could not be afforded, then bookshelves could be constructed in deal and painted a flat colour, possibly 'Indian red or a blueish green ... relieved by patterns and borders of white or yellow'. As a warning Eastlake added that, 'in all chromatic decoration ... bright and violent hues en masse should be avoided'. Only the lower shelves should be enclosed by cupboard doors, offering 'excellent closets for pamphlets and manuscripts' (Downing), and ornamented with brass or iron hinges and escutcheons.

Eastlake also suggested that the frieze at the top of the bookcase between the books and the cornice could be

Library desks, secretaires and bookcases were often extravagantly ornate, taking on an almost ecclesiastical appearance. Busts of learned scholars placed on top of a simple bookcase, like the one designed by Loudon (right), were recommended as a source of decoration by Downing, while Talbert's Reformed Gothic library (left) is full of illuminated manuscripts, lecterns, busts and rich decorative details.

'decorated with painted ornament in the form of arabesques, armorial bearings, and appropriate texts', whereas Downing said that 'busts of distinguished men, in different departments of letters, may be so placed along the top to designate to what particular class of books the space directly below is allotted'. The pilasters separating each compartment could also be treated in a complementary way.

Even in smaller houses without a separate library, hanging bookshelves and corner bookcases in the simplest of Gothic styles were to be found and were usually situated in the back parlour or the dining room.

Again, large fireplaces and chimneypieces were a focal point of the room. Medieval themes, heraldry and Gothic motifs were displayed on them, and Burges's chimneypiece for the library at the Tower House was even shaped like a castle (see page 15 for his similar design for Cardiff Castle).

Chapter 4
Kitchens & Bathrooms

'A good kitchen … should be erected with a view to the following particulars.
1. Convenience of distribution in its parts, with largeness of dimension.
2. Excellence of light, height of ceiling, and good ventilation. 3. Easiness of
access, without passing through the house. 4. Sufficiently remote from the
principal apartment … 5. Plenty of fuel and water, which … should be so near
it, as to offer the smallest possible trouble in reaching them.'

Mrs Beeton, Book of Household Management *(1861)*

The kitchen in a Victorian Gothic house would not have differed from that of any other style of Victorian home, and today it would be impractical to try to recreate an exact replica of a nineteenth-century kitchen without the convenience of state-of-the-art appliances and the demands of modern standards of hygiene. However, the 'feel' of a Victorian kitchen can be achieved by blending contemporary machinery with antique furniture, displays of crockery and utensils, and the addition of many period features that are now being widely reproduced by manufacturers.

In terraced houses the kitchen was originally situated in the basement; then, in the 1870s, basements began to disappear, safer stoves were produced, plumbing techniques were improved and gas began to be installed. As the risk of fire was now reduced, kitchens were therefore moved upstairs to a rear extension of the house. However, in most Gothic Revival houses, with their individual, asymmetrical plans and their lack of a basement area, the kitchen was always placed on the ground floor adjoining the dining room, but distant from the other principal reception rooms.

While the mistress of the house was viewed by Mrs Beeton as the 'superintendent' of her servants, supervising the domestic and financial arrangements of the household, the kitchen, which was a hive of activity from dawn to dusk, was ruled by the cook, on whom the 'whole responsibility of the business of the kitchen rests'.

With few labour-saving devices, the layout of the kitchen was dominated by the large cooking range and the central wooden kitchen table, on which most of the food preparation took place and around which the servants ate their meals. According to Mrs Beeton, the kitchen table 'should be massive, firm and strongly made … The upper surface of the table board should be

Romsey Cabinetmakesrs

Smallbone of Devizes

THIS PAGE AND OPPOSITE: *Because Victorian kitchens did not reflect the nineteenth-century 'battle of styles', it was features such as arched windows and* chimney-breasts that gave them their distinctive Gothic look. Antique jelly moulds and other equipment assist in giving an authentic touch to a modern kitchen.

kept well scrubbed; the edge of the table board, the frame and the legs should be stained and varnished.' Drawers were optional, and drop wings were to be avoided as they were considered unstable. Some tables had a shelf (a pot-board) between their legs on which large pots and pans were stored, while other kitchen utensils hung from a rectangular frame above the table. A heavy iron chandelier placed in the centre of the ceiling lit the room.

It was essential for the kitchen to work efficiently as there were usually several servants doing chores in the room at the same time. The kitchen therefore also contained other furniture, including smaller wooden side tables, a marble-topped table for rolling pastry, some simple chairs, a corner cupboard and a large wooden dresser on which crockery, jars and spice boxes were displayed. The dressers were usually built into the room, ranged along a wall or fitted into an alcove, and were often painted in chocolate brown or bottle green. Linen and cutlery were stored in the drawers, and bulkier items, such as bread bins and large storage jars, were placed in the deep cupboards – or on an open shelf – underneath.

Before the introduction of the stove, cooking was done over an open hearth, but from the late 1700s, cooking and heating began to be combined in a cast-iron range, which had a central grate with an open coal fire, an oven for baking on one side and a tank to heat water on the other. Pots and kettles were suspended over the fire by a crane, and food was roasted on a spit in front of the fire.

Thanks to technological improvements, a closed stove was developed, which, by the 1840s, came into more general use rather than just in the homes of the wealthy. These new stoves were at first bewildering to cook on. When a large, cast-iron stove was installed in the White House kitchen in the 1850s, the President himself had to consult the patent office to discover how it worked as the cook was unable to master the newfangled contraption. The new stoves were more efficient because, being airtight, they did not need to be refuelled so often, and they were safer because sparks were contained within them. Originally run on wood, stoves were soon being fuelled by coal, as supplies became cheaper owing to improvements in rail transport. The first appearance of a gas stove was at the Great Exhibition in 1851, although it was not widely available until much later.

Everyday kitchen items provided decoration, including arrays of china on the dresser and gleaming copper lids hung above the fireplace.

Food was stored in a cool pantry off the kitchen, away from the heat of the range, or, until the first refrigerators were introduced in the 1860s, preserved in an ice-house situated either on a back porch or in an underground tank. There would also be a scullery where the sink was placed and where the washing-up and laundry were done. The sink was normally positioned under a window, and made of white or brown glazed

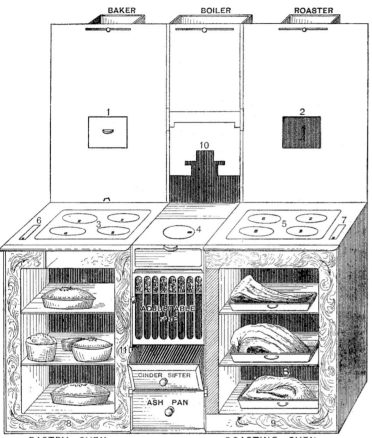

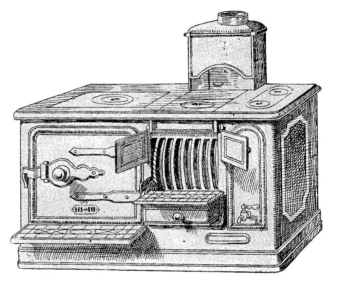

The range was the focal point of the kitchen, not only for the vast amount of cooking that took place to feed large Victorian families and to cater for their love of entertaining, but also to provide heat. The Book of the Home, published c. 1870, showed some of the new styles of stove available.

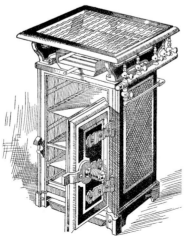

stoneware with a wooden draining board on either side. Larger houses would also have a butler's pantry between the kitchen and the dining-room, where glass and silver were kept in glass-fronted cupboards and where food was decorated before being served. Today's kitchens do not normally have these additional rooms and their functions now have to be combined into a single space.

The décor of the Victorian kitchen was very simple as there were no ornate architectural details in this part of the house. Walls needed to be washed down regularly for hygienic reasons, and so painted surfaces predominated. Plain colours such as white, grey, cream and beige were used, although some contemporary American source books suggested the use of bolder shades such as yellow

Robinson & Cornish

Robinson & Cornish

Underwood

Martin Moore

Many companies today produce a wide range of Victorian-style kitchens which combine modern appliances and convenience with nineteenth-century decorative details. Tiles inset into chimney-breasts, hanging pots and pans, and dried herbs, displayed china and a kitchen range all enhance the period flavour.

Chalon UK Ltd

Shortland

and dark red. Kitchen walls often had wainscoting around them – panels of soft wood grained to look like mahogany or oak – as well as a plate rail about 30 centimetres (1 foot) below the level of the ceiling, which provided additional storage as well as a decorative feature.

Floors were usually of hardwood, which was either oiled and varnished or painted, or of stone or tiles, which were then covered with rag rugs or decorated oil-cloths. They could then be swept and washed regularly so that hygiene was maintained.

A modern kitchen in a Victorian Gothic house can enjoy the conveniences of today's technology and yet still reflect the flavour of the period. Gothic details such as the pointed arch, found on the doors and windows of the house, can be copied on the fronts of kitchen cupboards, and these can either be specially made or bought from one of the ranges of the many kitchen companies that now specialise in reproducing Victorian designs. To keep true to the style, cupboard doors should be of natural wood or painted. New equipment can be hidden behind cupboard doors or kept very simple so that it does not detract too much from the atmosphere of the room.

As a result of the proliferation of antique shops and architectural salvage yards, much Victorian furniture and equipment has been rescued and restored. Such items add character to the kitchen. A large variety of original furniture can still be found – wooden dressers, corner cupboards, sideboards, plate racks, pie safes (free-standing cupboards with perforated wire windows to protect food from flies), kitchen tables and chairs – which will make the kitchen an inviting room rather than a purely functional space. The skill is to track down individual pieces with Gothic features on them. If antiques are difficult to find – or too expensive to buy – an alternative is reproduction furniture, which is now widely available. Displays of colourful crockery and glassware, as well as a collection of everyday Victorian utensils, will add authenticity.

Reproduction kitchen ranges with all mod cons are now very fashionable and are sold in most kitchen shops and department stores, although they are more expensive than a normal oven. Original cast-iron ranges can also still be found, but they need to be carefully checked by an expert and reconditioned before use. Nowadays they are usually used as a decorative feature, often inset into a fireplace, with a more conventional cooking appliance placed elsewhere in the room.

Porcelain or stoneware butlers' sinks, wooden draining boards or a wooden plate rack above the sink for drainage, brass taps and original Victorian tiles around the sink or behind the oven all add atmosphere to the kitchen. A plain brass chandelier in the centre of the room and simple muslin curtains – or blinds if the windows are pointed – will complete the scene.

The Book of the Home *gave Victorians tips on what to have in their houses. Here a selection of 'new' kitchen equipment is shown, including a fridge (left) and a milkshake maker (opposite, bottom far right).*

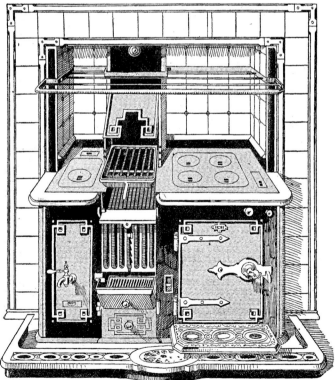

Skillet or Stew-pan
with three legs.*

Gridiron:
Fry-pan Pattern.*

Pot Digester.*

Double Sauce-pan.*

Dean's Patent Grilling Pan.*

Set of Copper Bain-Marie
Pans.†

The Queen's Pudding Boiler (no cloth used).§

Open.   Closed.

Gourmet Boiler
(stands inside
sauce-pan).§

Nest of Sanitary Seamless
Steel Sauce-pans and
Covers (handles loose).†

Sanitary Seamless Steel
Fish Fryer, with wire
drainer.†

Sanitary Seamless Steel Steamer.†

*T. & C. Clark & Co.
Wolverhampton.
† W. Sugg & Co., Ltd.
London, W.C.
§ Gourmet & Co.
London, W.C.

Brough's Patent "Lucky Kettle".*

Heritage Bathrooms

The Victorians' love of decoration extended to the bathroom, and shining wooden toilet seats and ornamental legs on roll-top baths embellished sanitary fittings, while pictures and chairs furnished the room. A modern bathroom (opposite) complements a Gothic house by the clever use of arches and panelling.

Bathrooms

Before the 1870s, when a circulatory hot-water system was developed, houses did not have separate bathrooms. Instead, servants brought buckets of hot water upstairs and filled jugs with it, which they then poured into portable bathtubs placed in the bedroom. People were therefore able to wash themselves in the privacy of their bedrooms, keeping warm in front of the fire.

Nor did many homes have inside water closets. Although some better residential districts had a piped water supply for part of the day, by 1855 only one in ten houses in London was linked to a proper sewer, and it was not until the mid-1860s that Sir Joseph Bazalgette's

plans for a sewage removal system for the whole of London was completed. Thomas Cubitt, the builder of more luxurious homes, claimed that all the houses he built after 1824 had their own water closet, but the average new suburban house did not have one until the 1880s. Also, until the 1880s plumbing techniques were not good enough to allow water closets to be fitted on an upper storey. Therefore, until the late nineteenth century, outdoor privies, earth closets or chamberpots were the norm.

With today's sanitary requirements, it is therefore impossible to recreate an exact replica of a Victorian Gothic 'bathroom', but modern bathrooms can easily

be designed to complement a Gothic home and conjure up the atmosphere of a typical nineteenth-century room.

Like the kitchen, the bathroom of a Victorian Gothic house was no different from that in any other Victorian home. Changes in appearance and efficiency of sanitary equipment were not dictated by architectural purity and design, but by considerations of hygiene and technological improvements.

Until the 1870s baths were portable, not fixed, and made of cast iron. The most common baths were shallow ones – shaped like an oval dish – for sponging oneself down; iron or zinc hip-baths, which had high, sloping backs and were deep enough to submerge most of the body; sitz-baths, which were either oval or square with a small seat; and portable showers, which looked like a tent and poured water on to the bather from a tank at the top. Designs for bathtubs were varied – and often quite decorative – and at the Great Exhibition a wide range was on display.

Gothic architects did occasionally indulge their medieval fantasies even in the bathroom, but these only appeared in the most ornamented and extravagant commissions. William Burges was one such designer, placing a Roman marble bath in an alcove off a bedroom at Cardiff Castle inlaid with metal figures of fish, newts and an octopus, and lining the walls of another bathroom at the Castle with sixty different kinds of polished marble. Even one of the guest washstands in his own home, Tower House, had a bronze bull from whose throat the water poured into a basin inlaid with silver fish.

However, most Victorian homes did not have separate bathrooms until the late 1870s, after there were improvements in sewage and drainage systems and a heightened awareness of the importance of hygiene and cleanliness. Initially small bedrooms or dressing rooms were turned into bathrooms and thus retained the architectural features of the room, with decorative cornices, ceiling mouldings, wooden floors, and windows often with stained glass in them. Fireplaces were essential to provide ventilation as well as warmth. Functional items such as bathtubs, washbasins and unsightly pipes were hidden within wooden pieces of furniture, and rugs, mirrors, cane-seated chairs, washstands, wooden towel rails, pictures, plants and even sofas were added to make the room seem like any other in the house. These bathrooms were usually decorated with dark, patterned wallpapers, which hid water stains. Whereas in houses with sash windows bathrooms would have had prettily gathered curtains, the narrow, pointed windows found in the Gothic Revival home were more suited to simple blinds.

By the end of the century, when the link between health and cleanliness was more widely known, hygiene in bathrooms became paramount. Pipes and sanitary equipment were now exposed so that they could be

OPPOSITE: *The Vita Nuova washstand created by Burges for his guest bedroom at the Tower House. One visitor described it thus: 'A fine bronze which most of us would place on some table, here makes itself useful – a bull from whose throat ajar pours into a Brescia basin ... How do you get the water in? See you that other bronze, a tortoise ... it is a plug; twist him round and the bull fills the basin.'*

THIS PAGE: *Until changes in hygiene requirements ruled that pipes should be exposed, bathroom fittings were encased in heavy wood-panelled structures.*

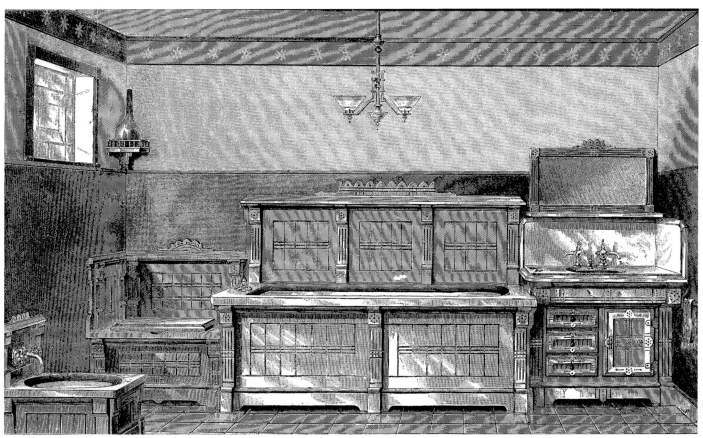

Highly decorative, original Victorian fittings reconditioned for modern use (opposite), or good reproduction ones (right), give a bathroom authenticity. Gothic-arched mirrors and decorative panels add a finishing touch.

cleaned more easily, and tiles were used on floors and walls, usually up to a dado rail, so as to keep germs at bay. As a result, tile production grew rapidly, and cheaper tiles soon became more widely available. However, they were still relatively expensive, and many suburban bathrooms had linoleum or 'cork carpet' on the floors instead, with additional mats or cork boards to absorb any puddles.

Fixed bathrooms became more common after 1870 once new technology made it possible for hot water to be piped round the house by means of a water tank placed on an upper storey. The tank was usually in an airing cupboard on the floor where the bedrooms were situated, and the water was then heated by the range in the kitchen below. Fixed baths, usually of cast iron, with white porcelain enamel interiors, were at first encased in wood panelling and edged with tiles. However, for reasons of hygiene, they were replaced in the 1880s with free-standing, rolled-top baths, which were raised from the floor on claw or ball feet so that the area underneath could be cleaned. Exposed copper or brass pipes that were polished regularly were introduced for cleanliness

but also became a decorative feature, as did the floral or stencilled patterns that appeared on the exterior of many bathtubs.

At the same time, washstands with decorative water jugs and bowls were replaced by fixed ceramic washbasins, which at first were called 'lavatories'. Originally inset into a marble-topped washstand or a wooden (usually mahogany) cabinet, with their pipes concealed, these large, often oval, basins were later supported by metal legs or ornate iron brackets, with their plumbing clearly visible, again for improved hygiene. Sink tops were also made of granite, slate and white porcelain. Tiles or marble provided practical splash-backs, and the insides of basins were often decorated with patterns to match those on the bath.

Taps were made of brass, nickel or porcelain, with cross-shaped or lever handles. Porcelain handles were sometimes painted with flowers, while ornamental stones, such as marble, coloured onyx and crystal, were occasionally used to decorate the tap.

Fixed showers did not appear in the bathroom until the very end of the nineteenth century and usually

The Water Monopoly

consisted of a simple brass showerhead, although some had 'needle sprays', which directed the water at different parts of the body.

Water closets were always placed in a room on their own, and until the end of the century were not part of the main bathroom. They were usually found in unventilated spaces on the ground floor of the house, but laws regarding hygiene were tightening up, and in 1875 an Act of Parliament ruled that they must have at least one outside wall and a window, as well as their own water supply and soil pipe connecting them to a sewer.

Although Joseph Bramah had invented a flushing water closet in 1778, it was so expensive and complicated to install, and used up such a large amount of water, that it could be afforded only by wealthier homes. More common was the Hopper water closet, which consisted of a funnel with a U-bend trap; later, an S-bend system was developed, into which water was poured through a hole in the side, resulting in the contents being swirled through the trap and into a drainpipe. However, until the middle of the nineteenth century most homes had only an outside privy situated on top of a cesspit, or an earth closet with dry earth or ashes underneath. Alternatively, they used chamber pots, which were emptied by the servants.

With the production of cast-iron or glazed earthenware pipes in the 1850s, new sewage disposal schemes in the 1860s, and the ability to pipe water around the house in the 1870s, internal plumbing soon improved. Overhead water storage tanks, in which waste was flushed away by water flowing quickly into the pan from a raised cistern, were developed in the mid-1870s, and by 1890 Thomas Crapper of Chelsea had invented the standard 'washdown' toilet. By 1895 the low-level cistern, still in use today, was introduced.

Like other bathroom fittings, water closets were at first hidden from sight, usually within a wooden box, but hygienic requirements soon dictated that toilets were exposed. For decoration, their glazed earthenware or porcelain bowls were often painted inside and out and supported on sculptured pedestals. The main manufacturers of these were Twyford and Doulton. Seats, supported by cast-iron brackets, were made of mahogany, polished walnut or pine, and cisterns and handles were of porcelain.

Today, original Victorian baths and basins can still be bought in architectural salvage shops, although often at considerable expense. If necessary, they can then be restored by specialists, who recondition fittings, pipework and taps and re-enamel the interiors of cast-

Manufacturers' catalogues displayed the very latest bathroom designs. Baths and showers were hidden inside wood-panelled frames, often carved with some kind of architectural detail.

iron baths. Nowadays, however, reproduction Victorian baths and basins, as well as brass taps, are widely manufactured and are usually more efficient and easier to maintain than original ones, although modern baths are slightly shorter than Victorian tubs, and basins too are smaller. Victorian toilets, cisterns and other accessories can also still be found, but reproduction sanitaryware, with the advantages of modern pipework and plumbing, are manufactured today by a large number of firms and are more practical to use and economical to install than 'antique' versions.

Accessories with Gothic features can be added to complement the bathroom of a Gothic Revival home; for example, as in the kitchen, cupboard doors can be made with panels in the shape of a pointed arch; tiles and stained-glass windows with Gothic motifs can be obtained; and even chairs and plant holders designed in Gothic shapes can enhance the feel of the room.

Chatsworth Bathrooms Limited

Heritage Bathrooms

ABOVE AND ABOVE RIGHT: *Gothic details on panelling and stained-glass windows provide simple decorative treatments to these bathrooms.*

RIGHT: *An imaginative scheme makes dramatic use of the Gothic arch.*

OPPOSITE LEFT: *Tiles were a major feature of Victorian decoration and were used in bathrooms for embellishment as well as for hygienic reasons. These are a selection of American Gothic designs.*

Ideal Standard

Imperial Bathrooms Company

Designs in Tile

ABOVE AND TOP CENTRE: *Decoration was found everywhere in the Victorian home, including the bases of toilets and as stencil designs on the side of baths. Even an insignificant washstand was given an element of appropriate detail.*

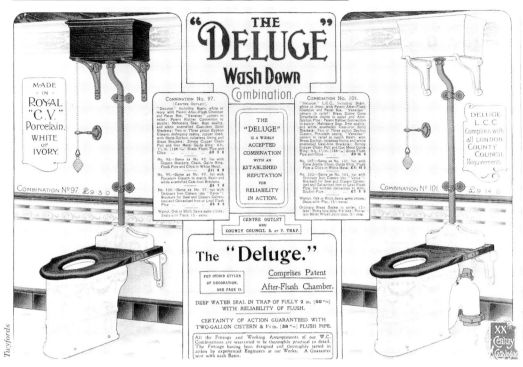

ABOVE: A contemporary advertisement for the latest in water closets.

Washstands with inset basins, and even toilets (below and bottom right), were treated as imposing pieces of furniture until the 1870s, when free-standing basins on pedestals or ironwork stands (opposite right and opposite below) became popular for reasons of hygiene.

Chapter 5
Interior Details

OPPOSITE: *The fireplace, with its elaborately carved chimneypiece, was the dominant feature of the Victorian Gothic living room.*

BELOW: *Medieval stained glass illustrated by Owen Jones in the* Grammar of Ornament. *Jones's book had a profound influence on design in the second half of the nineteenth century.*

'*The Gothic Style. The distinguishing characteristics of this style of interior finish are the prevalence of perpendicular lines, and the introduction, in all important openings, of the pointed arch, together with the use of the bold and deep mouldings that belong to its ornamental portions.*'

A. J. Downing, The Architecture of Country Houses

As George Gilbert Scott wrote in his *Remarks on Secular and Domestic Architecture*, 'In the interior of our houses we have even greater scope than externally for giving originality of character to our style, and for rendering it essentially our own, rather than a mere revival.' Therefore, despite the strict principles adhered to by Gothic Revival architects on the exterior of a house, the Victorians could richly embellish their interior walls, ceilings, floors and woodwork, especially in the rooms in which they entertained, and thus display to the world their varying degrees of social status and wealth.

As a reaction to eighteenth-century Gothick, with its ornamental sham decoration, Victorian Gothic interior details after Pugin concentrated on the structural beauty of a room rather than on plasterwork, although mass-produced plaster mouldings with Gothic motifs did appear on smaller suburban villas later in the century. Even Pugin complained of Gothic decoration in which 'every room ... must be fitted with niches, pinnacles, groining, tracery, and tabernacle work, after the manner of a chantry chapel ...' For him there was 'no repose' in these interiors: 'the whole is covered with trifling details, enormously expensive, and at the same time subversive of good effect'.

Charles Eastlake's best-selling *Hints on Household Taste* was one of the most influential books in the history of nineteenth-century interior design, and throughout the book he extolled the virtues of traditional methods of craftsmanship over mass-produced items. His ideas spread the principles of the Gothic Revivalists to a wider audience, and his suggestions for interior decoration soon became standard features in many Victorian homes.

Stuart Interiors

Although Pugin's interiors and furniture and those of later Gothic designers were inspired by medieval craftsmanship and patterns, those who today wish to achieve a Gothic feel in their homes can afford to be less purist about how they decorate their houses. Most architectural salvage companies stock antique panelling and floors, often taken from ecclesiastical sources, as well as doors, windows, stained glass, pews, fireplaces and metalwork – all of which can be incorporated into the interior of a Gothic house to provide atmosphere. Also, appropriate interior details can be purchased from the many manufacturers now reproducing a wide range of medieval and Gothic designs in wood, plasterwork and metal, as well as reviving many of the original patterns for textiles, wallpapers and tiles.

Walls

The predominant feature of any Gothic Revival house was its woodwork. Carved panelling on walls, doors and other internal structures echoed woodwork found in medieval buildings. In wealthier homes very expensive, full-height oak or mahogany panelling would be found on the walls of the entrance hall and the main reception rooms, especially the dining room and the library, while middle-class homes had panelling on the lower part of the wall only. The panels would be a simple linen-fold pattern, so popular in the fifteenth and sixteenth centuries, or in the shape of a Gothic arch, or richly carved with heraldic symbols, flowers and foliage or other medieval motifs. The panelling, or 'ancient woodwork', as Pugin wrote in *True Principles*, allowed 'large spaces left for hanging and tapestry'. In poorer homes, wainscoting – or imitation panelling – was a cheaper option.

As Scott pointed out, the woodwork in a house revived the skills of ancient joiners and was 'consistent with the style we are reviving, and with the usages of our own day'. It could then be carved to suit the owner of the house – for example, 'A person of antiquarian prepossessions may find pleasure in making his house rigidly medieval'. By freely applying 'the artistic style of our indigenous architecture' and 'subject to common sense', carved woodwork could then be adapted by a skilled joiner 'to our own requirement'.

In the early years of Victoria's reign, the wall, the cornice and the skirting board were treated as one area, although in the late 1830s Loudon was suggesting the addition of a dado rail in a very high-ceilinged room. By the 1870s Eastlake was advocating in his *Hints on Household Taste* that walls should be divided into three – the tripartite wall – with a dado, or 'plinth space of plain colour', rising to a height of 1-1.2 metres (3-4 feet) from the floor, a frieze just below the ceiling and wallpaper hung in between. To complement the richness of the panelling, wallpapers filling the central part of

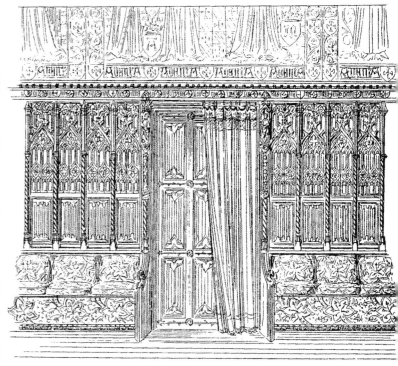

the wall were in strong, flat patterns derived from medieval sources, as created by designers such as Pugin and Owen Jones (see pages 129-34).

Wooden skirting boards were varnished and stained to 'add richness of tone' (Scott), and deep cornices joining the wall and the ceiling were heavily carved with trefoil or quatrefoil designs, tracery, Tudor roses or foliage, birds and, in one house, harriers in full chase. These cornices would often then be painted in colours that were lighter in tone, to pick them out from those used on the walls.

Ceilings

The common perception of a Gothic ceiling, with its soaring vaults of stone or wood inspired by medieval churches, was in reality to be found only in grand houses that had a private chapel or a great hall with its own roof. The plasterwork fan vaulting of eighteenth-century Gothick was derided by the Victorian Revivalists, who initially believed that ceilings should be constructional – i.e. showing the beams and joists supporting the floor above. These could then be embellished by moulding or carving the exposed timbers, or, as Scott suggests, 'by the use of beautiful corbels, and by the addition of painted decoration'. Downing also recommended 'rendering [the beams] somewhat ornamental by planing, chamfering, and beading them on the underside, and supporting them, where they join the side walls, by suitable and characteristic brackets'.

The high ceilings of Victorian houses, especially in the main rooms, were well suited to these decorative treatments. Whatever the ceiling, the aim of a Victorian Gothic one was to create a feeling of verticality that drew the eye upwards, rather than a flat, horizontal

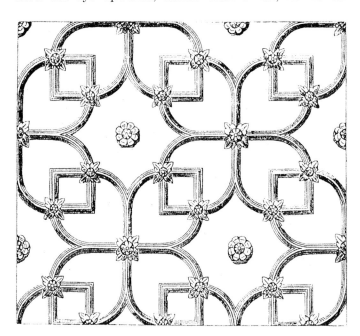

OPPOSITE: *In* True Principles, *Pugin showed two examples of 'ancient wood-work', 'more or less enriched with carving', which decorated the walls of a room. This 'mere panelling', hung with tapestries, was his ideal form of wall treatment.*

ABOVE RIGHT: *A design for a Gothic Revival ceiling with ornamental pendants at the intersection of the ribs, and Tudor rose motifs. This drawing appeared in C.J. Richardson's* Picturesque Designs for Houses, Villas, Cottages, Lodges, etc. *(1870).*

RIGHT: *The ceilings of two timbered houses which display 'the common floor joists and carrying beams',*

structural forms that Pugin believed were 'rendered exceedingly beautiful by moulding and carving'.

plane, which was the preferred look in neo-Classical homes. Apart from vaulting, this was achieved by a variety of effects including coffering (ornamental sunken square or polygonal panels), reminiscent of sixteenth-century ceilings, and the use of two inclined planes rising from the sides to the centre with the ribs showing (Downing here advocated the use of plaster ribs).

Scott also described three other kinds of acceptable ceiling: 'the partially constructive ceiling' which showed the beams but with wood panelling concealing the joists;

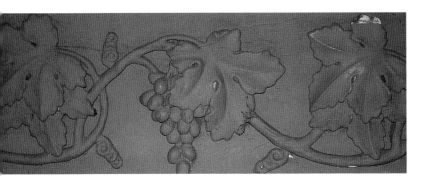

ABOVE: *A deep frieze at the top of a cornice, carved with a floriated design.*

RIGHT: *Plasterwork mouldings as a form of ceiling decoration were considered a sham by Gothic Revival architects.*

BELOW LEFT, CENTRE AND RIGHT: *Linenfold panelling, sometimes with elaborately carved panels above, and covering most of the wall, was the predominant style of wall decoration, especially in large urban villas, and country houses.*

'the non-constructive ceiling in which all the timbers are hidden by wood panelling'; and either of these two but with 'plaster substituted for boarding in the plain spaces within the panels, or the whole surface between the beams'. As far as Scott was concerned, this was the only legitimate use of plaster – a material which, unlike wood, reflected light and thus was 'pleasing' in a domestic setting. It was also a surface that could be lightly decorated, painted and gilded.

However, plasterwork did appear in many homes to provide Gothic features, especially from the 1850s when two inventions – flexible gelatine moulds, which produced projecting and undercut embellishments previously done by hand, and fibrous plaster, which was stronger and lighter – made it less expensive and therefore more widely available. This meant that even in smaller homes, plaster ribs and vaults could be applied across whole ceilings, and the areas in between could be adorned with heraldic motifs, pendants or bosses.

Overall ceiling decoration was the predominant feature of Gothic houses rather than just a decorative cornice and ceiling rose, overhead lighting being provided by a gleaming brass or ironwork chandelier hanging from the centre. The master of decorative ceilings was of course Burges, who, inspired by

astrology and Islamic sources as well as by medieval ones, created dazzling overhead theatrical effects. His multicoloured painted ceilings include signs of the zodiac, glittering stars, and the famous gilded 'jelly mould' panels in the dining room at Cardiff Castle, which are surrounded by low-relief panels carved to imitate pierced Islamic screens.

Internal Doors

Internal doors in Victorian Gothic houses, especially in the main living rooms, were usually tall, wide and wood-panelled. Hall doors, especially in halls rising to two storeys, were even more impressive than other doors in the house, being of elaborately carved or panelled wood with highly ornate, brass door furniture. Reception-

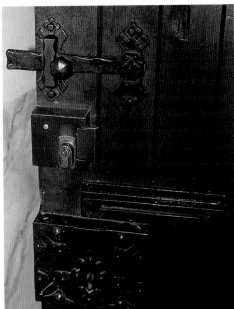

Imposing wooden doors with bold brass or metalwork hinges and finger plates were always the preferred style for the public rooms of a Victorian Gothic home.

room doors often had an architectural detail above them to complement the style of the house, and pointed-arch doorways were a common feature of many Gothic rooms. Oak, mahogany and other exotic hardwoods were the preferred material for these doors, but they were expensive and appeared only in wealthier homes and in the more public rooms of a house. The woods were varnished and sometimes stained.

White deal – a superior type of pine – was a cheaper alternative, as were woods such as pine and fir. They would be painted in a plain colour, but they were never grained to imitate better-quality woods, as the Gothic Revivalists considered this kind of finish a sham. As Scott wrote, the mouldings of these doors could be decorated with 'delicately designed enrichment, in simple lines and flat painting'.

Intricately worked door furniture completed the decoration. Pugin's particular interest lay in designing brass and wrought-iron lock-plates, 'finger' plates, door handles and hinges, which were created for him by John Hardman of Birmingham. Like Pugin, Hardman wanted to revive the forms and details of medieval metalwork, and produced most of the domestic and ecclesiastical metalwork that Pugin designed. As Pugin wrote in *True Principles*, 'hinges, locks, bolts were rendered in pointed architecture, rich and beautiful decorations'. Such ancient hinges, which 'extended the whole width of the door, and were bolted through in various places', were not only pleasing to the eye but, unlike modern hinges, could not be torn off easily.

Wrought iron had been used extensively in medieval times and Pugin followed the ancient practice of producing tinned or polychromatic ironwork rather than leaving it in the more common matt-black finish. His designs were inspired by locks and keys found on museum pieces, where 'ancient smiths' exercised 'the

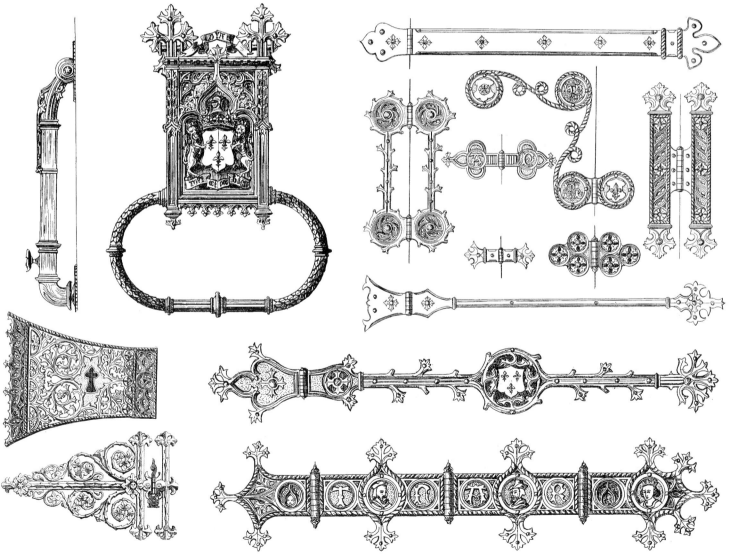

utmost resources of their art', and he included some very fine examples of these Gothic keys in the Medieval Hall at the Great Exhibition.

Interior Decoration

Loudon wrote in his *Encyclopaedia* that: 'The colouring of rooms should be an echo of their uses. The colour of a library ought to be comparatively severe; that of a dining room grave; and that of a drawing room gay. Light colours are most suitable for bedrooms.' Although the warm, rich tones of woods and sumptuous antique textiles convey the images of a Victorian Gothic interior, Scott rightly pointed out that 'the great principles of colouring are the same for all styles'. His only warning about decorating in the Gothic style was that 'no feeling of antiquarianism should be permitted to lead us to depart from the principles of sound taste'.

Pugin was one of the first architect/designers to create an entire decorative scheme for his interiors, and his two-dimensional, stylised patterns had a profound impact on designers throughout the second half of the nineteenth century. Improvements in chemical dyes in the 1850s, as well as the introduction of gas lighting in domestic interiors, meant that stronger, darker colours such as deep reds, sage green, Prussian blue and gold could be used. Medieval textiles, tapestries and illuminated manuscripts provided inspiration for decorative schemes, as did the Islamic patterns that can be seen in Burges's wildly colourful interiors. William Morris's bold, naturalistic designs for wallpapers and fabrics were greatly influenced by those of Pugin and other Gothic Revivalists, and his style became the embodiment of late Victorian décor.

Wallpapers

Two technological innovations revolutionised the growth of the wallpaper industry in early Victorian England. The first was the invention, in 1799, of Nicholas Louis

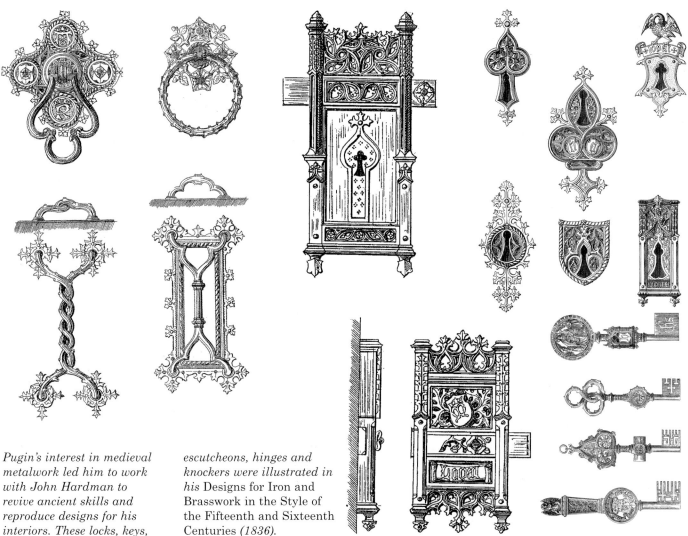

Pugin's interest in medieval metalwork led him to work with John Hardman to revive ancient skills and reproduce designs for his interiors. These locks, keys, escutcheons, hinges and knockers were illustrated in his Designs for Iron and Brasswork in the Style of the Fifteenth and Sixteenth Centuries *(1836).*

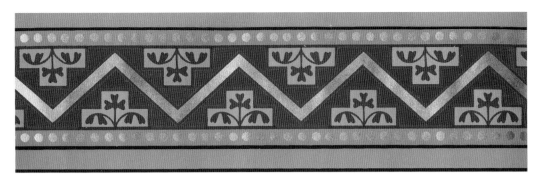

The publication of Pugin's Floriated Ornament *and* Owen Jones's The Grammar of Ornament *coincided with technological improvements and revolutionised wallpaper design in the mid-nineteenth century. Pugin's use of leaves and flowers, flattened into two-dimensional patterns, and Jones's repeating motifs and diaper (diamond) and geometric shapes, as well as other Gothic symbols such as the quatrefoil and the cross, became very fashionable and are still reproduced today. Pugin's 'Gothic Lily' wallpaper (opposite below left) was originally designed for the House of Commons.*

Bradbury & Bradbury Art Wallpapers

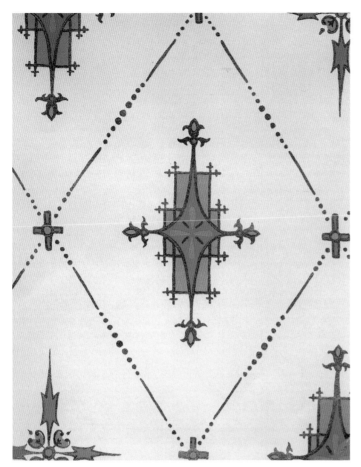

Robert's paper-making machine, the Fourdrinier, which formed a continuous roll of paper that could be cut to any length. Previously, individual sheets had had to be handmade from cotton, linen or woollen rags that had been reduced to a pulp by being suspended in water, drained, pressed between felts and then dried and bundled into reams. The sheets of paper were then glued together to form long strips, decorated with distemper paint to provide a background colour and then printed with a design carved on wood blocks. More delicate lines then had to be hand-painted on.

In 1841 Potters of Darwin in Lancashire perfected a steam-powered machine that printed wallpapers using cylinders with raised patterns. This early rotary printing press could produce 420 rolls an hour of two-colour paper, compared to the 300 rolls a day that a good craftsman could print by hand. New inks were developed to flow smoothly on to the new presses and coat the paper more thinly, which led to the possibility of printing larger-scale designs with wider repeat patterns, details that the earlier presses were not able to achieve.

Rolls of wallpaper were soon being commercially manufactured and, as their prices came down, were quickly adopted as the preferred form of wall decoration in most Victorian households. Early designs included flowers, plants, birds, trellis-work and French-inspired three-dimensional pictorial scenes of landscapes, architectural subjects and historical events.

Pugin, however, whose influence on wallpaper patterns was as dramatic as the new technology, was scornful of these designs because they denied the two-dimensional reality of a flat wall. Of patterns emulating Gothic motifs, he wrote: 'I will commence with what are termed Gothic-pattern papers ... where a wretched caricature of a pointed building is repeated from the skirting to the cornice in glorious confusion – door over pinnacle and pinnacle over door.' He also criticised false shading on wallpapers, claiming that, 'as a paper is hung around a room, the ornament must frequently be shadowed from the light side'. To disguise a solid wall surface with a three-dimensional pattern was a sham, and his flat-patterned designs, which made no attempt to show shadows or natural gradations of colour, were innovatory. The flock papers he designed were, he believed, an 'admirable substitute' for the wall-hangings and tapestries found on medieval walls, and their patterns 'without shadow, [but] with the forms relieved by the introduction of harmonious colours' conformed with the principles put forward in his book *Floriated Ornament* (see page 13).

For Pugin, the main fault of early Victorian decoration was its lush, rounded naturalism, a style he heavily criticised in *Floriated Ornament*. As he wrote, medieval craftsmen did not embellish their work with natural leaves and flowers, but with flat, stylised forms. For 'It is impossible to improve on the works of God; and

the natural outlines of leaves, flowers, etc. must be more perfect and beautiful than any invention by man ... the great skill of the antient artists was in the *adaptation* and *disposition* of their forms.'

His inspiration came not only from the stylised flowers and fruits found in illustrated medieval manuscripts, but also from heraldic emblems, the diaper (diamond) pattern 'employed during the Middle Ages for surface-decoration, and of which, perhaps, the Early Italian school of painting affords the best examples' (Eastlake), and other Gothic motifs. He also found ideas for designs from fifteenth-century velvet brocades and stencilled work.

The man who helped Pugin implement his wallpaper designs was John Gregory Crace, who had not only to organise their production but also to develop his sketches into working drawings. Over their long collaboration, Crace interpreted Pugin's designs and often selected their colours and fine-tuned the details. Despite all the new technology, Pugin's papers had to be hand-printed and were therefore costly to produce.

Pugin designed wallpapers for his private clients and their large country houses, devising bold patterns that reflected the mottoes, family crests and other symbols relevant to each individual patron. For the Palace of

Westminster he produced over 100 patterns in different colours, each paper being suitable to its particular setting. State and public rooms had formal-patterned flock or gold-leafed papers, while housekeepers' rooms were hung with simple floral patterns. Pugin also designed papers for more general use, seeing the wider circulation of his patterns as a way of spreading the principles of the Gothic Revival. However, his wallpapers would have been beyond the purse of most ordinary customers. Nowadays, specialist firms are still hand-printing Pugin's designs, although at a cost, and his original patterns have recently been rehung in the restoration of certain apartments in the Houses of Parliament.

Pugin's contribution to interior decoration was revolutionary because, as Eastlake pointed out, 'his greatest strength as an artist lay in the design of ornamental detail'. Pugin's principles of architecture extended to the question of ornament, which, he wrote, 'signifies the embellishment of that which is useful, in an appropriate manner'. By contrast – or, as he claimed, 'by a perversion of the term' – ornament 'is frequently applied to mere enrichment, which deserves no other name than that of unmeaning detail, dictated by no rule but that of individual fancy or caprice'.

What Pugin therefore attempted to do in *Floriated Ornament* was to lead designers 'back to first principles'.

By the mid-1850s, however, medieval patterns were being replaced by more geometric designs, influenced by the publication of Owen Jones's *The Grammar of Ornament* in 1856, with its colour illustrations of ornamentation around the world. Jones featured Moorish, Classical and Oriental patterns as well as medieval and Gothic ones, and these flat, repeating motifs and geometric shapes in strong primary colours soon began to appear on wallpapers.

At the same time, gas lighting meant that walls previously lit solely by candles could be covered with darker papers, allowing the deep, rich colours associated with the Victorian era to be widely adopted.

Wallpapers also began to be seen as a background to pictures and furniture, rather than as a strong decorative statement in their own right. When choosing wallpaper for a room, Eastlake wrote in *Hints on Household Taste* that if it was to be a mere backdrop, 'the paper can hardly be too subdued in tone. Very light stone colour or green (not emerald), and silver-grey will be found suitable for this purpose, and two shades of the same colour are generally sufficient for one paper. In drawing-rooms, embossed white or cream colour, with a

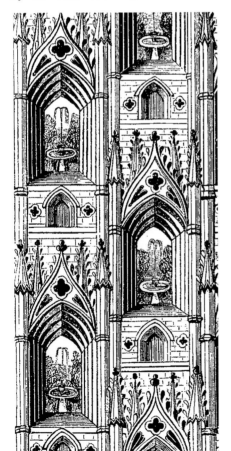

OPPOSITE: *An example of a tripartite wall scheme published in* The Book of the Home.

FAR LEFT: *In* True Principles, *Pugin called this kind of three-dimensional contemporary Gothic wallpaper design 'a wretched caricature'.*

LEFT: *Some of Christopher Dresser's wallpaper designs. Dresser acknowledged the influence that Pugin had had on his work.*

very small diapered pattern, will not be amiss, where water-colours are hung. As a rule, the simplest patterns are the best for every situation ... In colour, wall-papers should relieve without violently opposing that of the furniture and hangings by which they are surrounded. There should be one dominant hue in the room, to which all others introduced are subordinate ...'

From the 1840s, writers on interior decoration recommended using wallpaper in the better rooms of a house. The walls should be papered from the skirting board to the cornice, with a border as ornamentation. In North America, however, critics like Downing favoured architectural papers – fresco-papers – which imitated columns, friezes, and so on, and created

architectural elements in a room where none existed. These papers often accompanied scenic papers, which were very common in America.

Downing was a great advocate of the use of wallpaper, writing in 1850 that: 'Paper-hangings offer so easy, economical, and agreeable a means of decorating or finishing the walls of an apartment, that we strongly recommend them for use in the majority of country houses of moderate cost.'

Eastlake also believed that 'the more recent invention of paperhangings supplies a cheaper, readier, and, to our English notions of comfort, a more satisfactory means of internal decoration'. Recognising Pugin's contribution to wallpaper manufacture, he

wrote that: '[Pugin] led the way by designing some excellent examples for the Houses of Parliament and elsewhere; and since his time many architects have thought it worth while to design appropriate wallpapers for the houses which they have built. By degrees manufacturers took the matter up, and adopted the patterns suggested by qualified artists, and the result is that good and well-designed papers may now be had at a very reasonable price.'

Eastlake also suggested that embossed paper 'after the manner of old stamped leather' could be effective, but admitted that this 'mere imitation of leather ... is hardly consistent with principles illumined by what Mr Ruskin calls the Lamp of Truth'. However, as 'the manufacture of paperhangings is essentially a modern art ... [it] would be hypercritical therefore to prescribe any limits to its adaptation for decorative purposes beyond those which are necessarily imposed by the nature of the material and the process of manufacture. To go further than this in any branch of art would lead

to a sort of aesthetic Pharisaism.' Designers like Burges went as far as producing coordinating papers for all three sections of the tripartite wall, with angled versions for staircase walls.

Curtains and Upholstery

The heavily draped curtains and fussy upholstery that were so popular during the first half of the nineteenth century were a complete anathema to Pugin and the Gothic Revivalists. For Pugin, the 'true' use and intention of a curtain, suspended across a window, was purely to 'exclude cold and wind'. As curtains did not need to be drawn all the time, and should be 'opened and closed at pleasure', they needed only to be fixed 'to rings sliding on rods' with a wooden box at the top 'in front of which a valance is suspended to exclude air'. These simple curtain treatments were suspended on decorative metal, brass or painted wood poles attached to the moulding or cornice at the top of the window. The valance – fabric hanging in vertical folds from the pole

OPPOSITE LEFT: *Pugin's designs for tiles produced by Minton in the 1840s reflected the patterns that were also found on his wallpapers and textiles. These were based on his thorough understanding of medieval ornament.*

OPPOSITE RIGHT: *Suggestions for decorative wall treatments published in the* Technical Educator.

RIGHT: *A selection of cast-iron curtain poles with Gothic motifs at each end.*

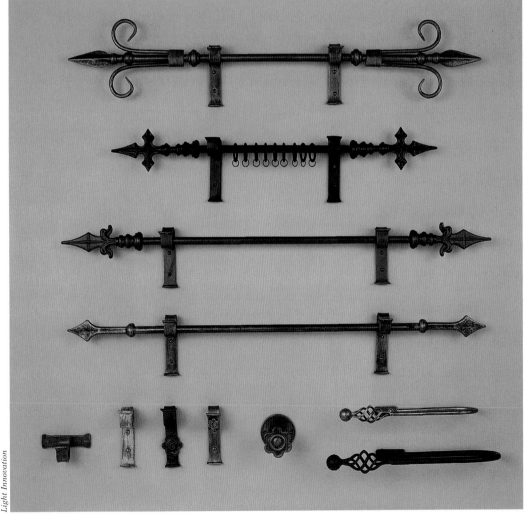

Light Innovation

or cornice – was attached by rings or hooks and hung below this but over the actual curtain, and then the curtain hung in front of the window, usually extending to the ground.

Materials could be 'rich or plain', 'lightly or heavily fringed', 'embroidered with heraldic charges or not, according to the locality where they are to be hung', but, in keeping with Pugin's *True Principles*, 'their real use must be strictly maintained'. Extravagant folds and festoons were condemned as 'abominable' taste, and were not only useless 'in protecting the chamber from cold' but were also 'the depositories of thick layers of dust … [and] the strong-holds of vermin'.

Fringing, which was originally 'nothing more than the ragged edge of the stuff, tied into bunches to prevent it unravelling further', should simply be of threads ' tied into ornamental patterns' and applied purely as an ornamental edging.

Pugin copied details from the antique textiles he had in his collection, and designed a whole range of fabrics in silk and damasks of cotton and wool to complement his interiors. He also turned for inspiration to the silks and velvets woven in Renaissance Italy, and many of his fabrics displayed traditional repeating patterns of pomegranates, artichokes, palmettes and stylised pineapples. Other curtain fabrics included crowned fleur-de-lys patterns, a serpentine design and a two-coloured rose-and-crown motif for a window blind in the House of Commons.

The Gothic Revivalists' reaction against the heavy drapery beloved by most Victorians on their curtains and upholstery was reinforced by Eastlake in the 1870s. He recommended simple curtain treatments and suggested that, as well as silk and damask, other materials such as cotelan (a mixture of silk and wool, often worked in a diaper pattern), cretonne (a substitute for chintz used in bed furnishings) and painted calico were acceptable alternatives. If curtains were changed in the summer months – a common Victorian practice – Eastlake suggested using 'Swiss lace' made of thread-cotton instead of the more popular muslin.

Portière curtains, which hung over doors to keep out draughts, could be made from more elaborate fabrics such as velvet and brocades decorated with deep borders, but their drapery should still be simple.

Furniture upholstery was also less ornate than that of other Victorian styles. Simple oak or mahogany frames were covered with antique brocades, velvets and specially designed fabrics and then trimmed with plain silk fringes. As medieval chairs did not have padded seats or backs, Pugin had to design leather ones based on seventeenth-century Spanish or Flemish styles in order for his chairs to be more comfortable. The heavily stuffed and rounded sofas found in many Victorian homes were rejected by the Gothic Revivalists; instead, Eastlake extolled the design and comfort of a

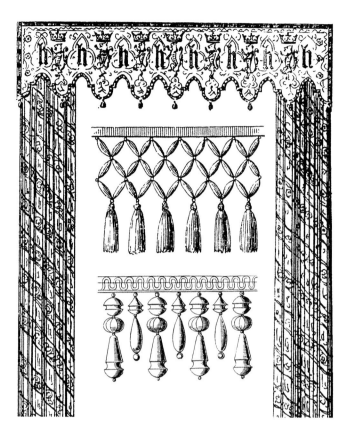

seventeenth-century sofa and chairs found at Knole House covered originally in a rose-coloured velvet, with panelled backs and seats trimmed with woven gold and silk thread, and decorated horizontally with a knotted fringe of the same material. These, he noted, 'without assuming the padded lumpy appearance of a modern armchair', were both 'sumptuous' and comfortable.

Flooring

Although most Victorian homes had carpets in their main rooms, thanks to improvements in machine-weaving, which made them cheaper, the predominant image of the flooring in Victorian Gothic houses is of polished hardwood covered with exotic rugs. In fact, except in wealthier homes, which could afford expensive hardwoods, most floors were of tongue-and-grooved softwood, which was either covered with a thin layer of parquet flooring which looked like hardwood or was strewn with rugs. More modest wooden floors were painted, stencilled or covered with mats, oil-cloth (a painted and varnished canvas) or drugget, an inexpensive coarse cloth. These were all hard-wearing, inexpensive and easy to keep clean.

Where rooms were carpeted, they were rarely fitted from wall to wall. Usually a 60-centimetre- (2-foot-) wide margin of floorboards was left around the edge of the room and decorated with patterned parquetry, painted or stained. Eastlake recommended that carpets should be 'left square at the sides', for, he believed, 'no one wants a carpet in the nooks and corners of a room'. These decorative wooden borders also allowed 'the nature of construction' to be seen, a prevailing principle in Victorian Gothic architecture and design.

OPPOSITE ABOVE*: Pugin's example of an ancient curtain and fringing, which, in his view, were the epitome of 'good taste'; however, he regarded the beading shown below it with derision.*

OPPOSITE BELOW*: Downing's suggested style for a Gothic curtain with its wooden cornice, drapery or valance, and fabric.*

ABOVE AND RIGHT*: Two types of drapery for a Gothic window and portière illustrated in* The Book of the Home.

FAR RIGHT*: Eastlake's curtain and rod displayed a simple 'elegance and richness of design'.*

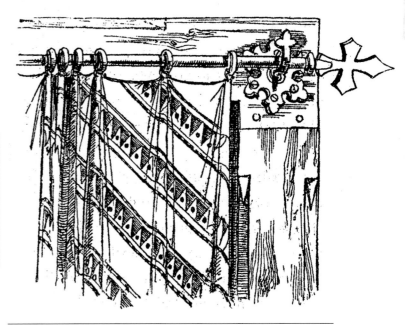

Scott also advocated enriching wooden floors by parquetry, 'and certainly floors thus ornamented, and only partially covered with carpets, add much to the beauty of a room'. Parquet flooring and decorative borders made up from different coloured hardwoods arranged in geometrical patterns were especially popular in England and the United States from the 1870s, when rugs and carpets from the Orient flooded into the West as trade routes rapidly began to open up.

Eastlake believed that people should save up and buy a real carpet imported from Persia, Turkey or India rather than purchase one of the many cheap imitations that were soon being widely manufactured. The quality of the colours and the irregularity of the patterns were examples of 'the true spirit of good and noble design'. Even the 'humblest type of Turkey carpet' was preferable to an English copy.

As for carpet designs, Eastlake deplored the prevailing Victorian taste for a 'thousand-and-one pictorial monstrosities'. In reaction, and according to his principles of architecture, Pugin's carpet designs were stylised floriated patterns – in fact the only patterns, he

Langley Castle

Langley Castle

The most commonly held image of Victorian window decoration is of lavish drapes, often comprising as many as four layers of curtains. Victorian Gothic drapery, however, was much simpler in style, complementing rather than dominating the architectural features of the windows and the room.

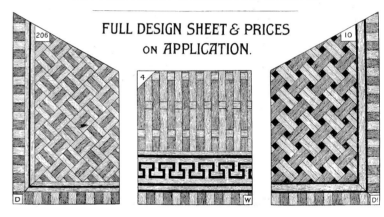

Oriental rugs newly imported from the East covered the polished wooden floors of the Victorian Gothic home. Parquetry (above top), made up of different coloured woods, was particularly popular.

believed, suitable for a flat surface like a floor. When writing in *True Principles* about modern carpets, 'the patterns of which are generally shaded', he declared: 'Nothing can be more ridiculous than an apparently reversed groining to walk upon, or highly relieved foliage and perforated tracery for the decoration of a floor.' His range of hand-knotted and machine-woven carpets complemented his interiors and wallpapers, and his designs for Brussels carpeting – with its heavy pile formed by uncut loops of wool – and for velvet-pile carpets, which were produced by Crace, received a prize at the 1851 Great Exhibition. After Pugin's death Crace continued to manufacture carpets based on his sketches.

Eastlake also suggested simple diapered patterns in a contrasting colour to the wallpaper. 'Large sprawling patterns,' he wrote, 'should be avoided as utterly destructive of effect to the furniture which is placed on them, and, above all, every description of shaded ornament should be sternly banished from our floors.'

Scott believed that 'Floors are too much lost sight of in modern houses as a field of decoration' and suggested that various coloured stones or marbles be used in halls and other paved areas, 'relieved by mosaic-work or encaustic tiles [see below]'. Another form of decoration was for incised patterns to be cut into stone or marble and then 'filled in with coloured cements'. These designs could be geometrical or floriated, but they could also 'contain figures or groups drawn with any degree of refinement, the only condition being that they must be in lines, as on an encaustic tile or Greek vase, and that the design should convey the idea of the smallest possible amount of relief'. Later, extravagantly designed and multicoloured marble and mosaic floors were a feature of Burges's imaginative interiors.

Tiles

Tiles were also an important feature of the Victorian home. They were hard-wearing and practical and lent themselves readily to decoration. The growth in tile manufacture during the nineteenth century by such firms as Minton and Doulton led to the use of tiles as flooring, inset into walls in hallways, kitchens and bathrooms, and as embellishments for fireplace surrounds, washstands, pieces of furniture and other decorative items such as flowerpots.

The most important form of tiling to be developed in the nineteenth century was encaustic (patterned) tiles, made by inlaying coloured clay into a terracotta ground. They were first manufactured in the 1840s and were originally used on the floors of Victorian houses. Expensive to produce, they appeared in the homes of the aristocracy and soon became highly fashionable. Combined with quarry and geometric (plain) tiles in order to reduce the cost, they were used to cover large areas such as entrance halls, porches, conservatories

Wall hangings such as these by Christopher Dresser adorned the walls of Reformed Gothic homes.

and garden paths. Middle-class homes then copied the style, but in cheaper forms and smaller areas; for example, hall floors using only geometric tiles became very popular. Clay tiles of red and different tones of brown and buff were the most common colours, but sometimes a more expensive white or blue tile would be added to the pattern.

The importance of encaustic tiles in Gothic Revival homes was inspired by the relationship between Pugin and the porcelain manufacturer Herbert Minton, who pioneered the production of encaustic tiles in the 1840s. Pugin was a collector of medieval floor tiles, which he had found on his travels throughout England and northern France. Inlaid tiled pavements had adorned the floors of many medieval ecclesiastical buildings, but the art of monastic tile-making had ceased in the sixteenth century with the dissolution of the monasteries. Tiles were not used in domestic buildings

Medieval inlaid floor tiles, rediscovered by Pugin and reproduced, along with new patterns, by Minton from the 1840s, soon became the most popular form of flooring in Victorian entrance halls. Pattern books for these encaustic tiles, showing geometric designs in brown and buff colours, with contrasting decorative borders, were widely published. Encaustic tiled floors in the halls of Gothic Revival homes were often complemented by dark oak panelling on the walls.

them, which had begun to appear in books on architecture in the 1840s. Other sources included stories from the novels of Walter Scott; Pugin's *Floriated Ornament*; Gothic motifs such as fleurs-de-lys and trefoil patterns, heraldry, coats of arms and calligraphy in the form of letters of the alphabet – usually the initials of the client. Pugin produced individual designs for some of his clients, but he also contributed to Minton's pattern books from around 1850. As he wrote to Minton in 1852, 'I think my patterns and your workmanship go ahead of anything'.

Tiles sometimes formed part of a complex pattern, but they could also be complete in themselves. The 15-centimetre- (6-inch-) square tile was the most common, but other shapes included diamonds, circles and rectangles as well as squares of different sizes. The patterned tiles were bordered by either contrasting coloured tiles or plain red or black quarry tiles.

until a century later, but they were of plain, quarried stone, which only the wealthy could afford. Pugin, who wanted to reproduce a medieval-style, inlaid floor tile, was introduced to Minton as a possible manufacturer in about 1840.

The original process for making inlaid floor tiles was patented by Samuel Wright of Shelton in 1830. It involved pouring liquid clay into a moulded pattern, which produced a two-colour tile. Later, Richard Prosser used powdered clay to manufacture tiles. Minton bought a share of both these patents, and by 1842 had published his first catalogue, *Early English Tiles*.

The first designs were inspired by patterns found on medieval tiles – antique ones as well as illustrations of

America was importing English encaustic tiles by the 1850s, although this made them very expensive. However, by the 1870s US manufacturers had begun producing them themselves. From the 1850s encaustic tiles were being recommended as the flooring to be used in vestibules, entrances, halls and on verandas, and they even appeared on an octagonal staircase in a house in New Jersey in 1855. Downing recommended tiles in 'browns, enriched with patterns and figures of fawn or blue' because he felt that they were more durable and economical than carpets or 'floorcloths'. John Bullock, in *The American Cottage Builder* (1854), advocated their use because they were easy to clean and fireproof, while Gervase Wheeler, an English architect who practised in the United States, wrote in *Houses for People* (1855) that encaustic tiles 'enlivened' the home.

By 1868 Eastlake was writing in his *Hints on Household Taste* that: 'There can be little doubt that the best mode of treating a hall-floor, whether in town or country, is to pave it with encaustic tiles. This branch of art-manufacture ... has not only reached great technical perfection as far as material and colour are concerned, but aided by the designs supplied by many architects of acknowledged skill, it has gradually become a means of decoration which, for beauty of effect, durability, and cheapness, has scarcely a parallel.' While acknowledging Minton's role in reviving 'this ancient art', he recommended the tiles produced by Messrs Maw & Co. for their unrivalled 'rich variety of patterns'.

As well as encaustic tiles, Minton also produced a wide range of glazed tiles for more decorative items, which had heraldic and other medieval patterns on them. The firm's design for a medieval stove covered with tiles was a prominent feature of the Great Exhibition, as were its jardinières made of tiles and metalwork. Burges's interiors also made spectacular use of glazed tiles manufactured by W. B. Simpson and Sons. He used tiles on deep friezes, chimneypieces and floors, and the subjects he displayed included mythological scenes, stories from the Scriptures and a wide range of mythical as well as real animals.

The growth in the use of tiles by the Gothic Revivalists, and the rediscovery and expansion of traditional forms of tile manufacture, were a major influence on William Morris and the Arts and Crafts movement. Morris's naturalistic and heraldic patterns were very fashionable by the 1870s, and the vivid colours and Islamic motifs used on the tiles created by the famous ceramicist William de Morgan echoed those adorning the interiors of William Burges.

Fireplaces

The fireplace with its chimneypiece was the focal point of the Victorian room, providing heat and, as Scott wrote, offering the greatest opportunity 'for beauty of design and novelty of treatment'. This applied to all styles of Victorian house, but more so in the Gothic Revival interior where an imposing fireplace, inspired by those found in medieval baronial halls, could be ornamented with wonderful carved and painted decoration displaying a wide variety of Gothic motifs and subjects. Fireplaces were also an indication of the wealth of the household – an important status symbol in Victorian times – as a large fireplace with ornate decoration not only spelt affluence but also showed that the owners had enough servants to clean it and tend it.

In rural areas in England and America, log-burning fires and stoves were still predominant – a form of fuel that suited the open fireplaces and dog-grates favoured

Gothic forms of decoration appeared not only on the fireplace and chimneypiece but also on the grate and on the firedogs.

by the Gothic Revivalists. However, with technological improvements in the design of grates in the 1840s, and with the expansion of the railways, which made cheaper coal available in the towns and cities, coal-burning grates soon appeared as the standard method of heating in the urban home.

The imposing fireplaces and chimneypieces designed by Gothic Revival architects were of elaborately carved stone and wood, which at times dominated their interiors. These displayed heraldic symbols, Gothic motifs, pointed arches and gilded and painted decoration. For example, one of Pugin's fireplaces for Eastnor Castle, Herefordshire, has a painted genealogical tree on its chimneypiece, while Burges's chimneypiece in the summer smoking room at Cardiff Castle has a winged God of Love with parrots on his wrists sitting above a carved frieze showing the summer amusements of lovers. Burges's highly carved creations were produced for him by the sculptor Thomas Nicholls.

Scott identified several types of chimneypiece as suitable for a Gothic interior: one 'opening flat with the

Manorhouse Stone

Aga Rayburn

Rudloe Hall

Although heavily carved wooden fireplaces were appropriate in the large, wood-panelled rooms found in grander Gothic houses, today's more modest homes can create a Gothic feature in a room by fitting a simple stone fireplace with a pointed arch detail, sometimes with another medieval motif above.

wall, covered by a straight lintel, an arch or a lintel on brackets'; the same style but decorated 'by projecting pillars and panelled frieze, with a corniced shelf, or with some other kind of frontispiece framing the opening'; and the hooded chimneypiece, 'overhanging the opening, and supported on pillars or brackets, or both, and of an infinity of different designs, from the most simple form … to the richest design'. Additional decoration could be added by using different coloured marbles, mosaic work, encaustic tiles or carved or inlaid wood.

Modern marble fireplaces, which for Scott were mere boxes 'formed of the thinnest slabs of marble', were to be avoided. Instead, 'a simple design, with moderate but real substance' was infinitely preferable to 'an ostentatious display of smartness with artificial bulk'. Marble joinery was acceptable only 'as a means of introducing marbles of varied colour', and as an alternative he recommended using plain stone, which could if necessary be decoratively painted.

By the end of the nineteenth century, the medieval inglenook fireplace – with its large, recessed space beside the fire, in which there was often a built-in seat – reappeared as another popular type of fireplace suitable for the larger rooms of Gothic Revival and Arts and Crafts houses.

Although wood-burning grates were more suitable for Gothic-style fireplaces, by the middle of the century Scott was suggesting the coal-burning register stove, which overcame the problem of draughts and the emission of sulphurous fumes, as an acceptable one to be used in a Gothic town house. This could be ornamented with iron or polished steel and 'by the introduction of brass, or encaustic tiles or porcelain'. The parts most exposed to the fire should be of cast iron, leaving decorative wrought ironwork or bronze to adorn areas not directly subjected to the heat. However, brick or tiles were 'still more obviously suited to a Gothic house' than iron, especially in the country.

As for fire accessories, Pugin attacked the 'nightmare world' of much Victorian Gothic design, complaining that: 'The fender is a sort of embattled parapet, with a lodge-gate at each end; at the end of the poker is a sharp-pointed finial, at the summit of the tongs a saint.' Instead, he pointed out that medieval firedogs were usually ornamented with heraldry, with the finer parts worked 'in brass for relief of colour and richness of effect'; and it was this style that he recommended for a Gothic Revival fireplace.

Lighting

At the start of the Victorian era, candles and oil lamps were the only forms of illumination in a room, casting a warm glow over the dimly lit interior. After 1845, when the paraffin lamp was introduced, and especially from the 1850s, when the first gas-light fittings were

THIS PAGE AND OPPOSITE: *Ornamental stoves, fireplace surrounds and grates embellished with ornate Gothic details were on display in the Medieval* *Court at the 1851 Great Exhibition, which helped bring Gothic design to a larger public. Manufacturers' advertisements also made designs more widely known.*

available, internal lighting drastically improved. This had a radical effect on interior decoration. Gas pipes at first could be connected only to a ceiling or wall light, but gradually, via the use of a rubber tube, gas could also be supplied to table lamps. Electricity, an expensive and initially inefficient form of lighting, was not available for domestic use until the 1880s.

The large metalwork chandeliers found hanging in medieval baronial halls were a source of inspiration for the Gothic Revival home, and Pugin was especially interested in making chandeliers and candlesticks in a base metal in the same way as his Gothic predecessors had done, although his later designs were machine-made to achieve the effect he required. His successful collaboration with John Hardman soon inspired other firms to begin producing similar styles of metalwork.

Even at an early age Pugin had been sketching wall sconces and candlesticks to be made in brass, and he also experimented with the effect that his designs had on a room's illumination. For example, one particular

Light Innovations

Tempus Stet

Stuart Interiors

Stuart Interiors

Metalwork chandeliers and wall sconces in brass and wrought iron were the most common form of lighting in the Victorian Gothic room, inspired by ones found in medieval buildings. Originally lit by candles, their flickering light would have created a warm glow in the room. Today, original light fittings can still be found, which can then be adapted for electricity.

Smithbrook Iron Lighting

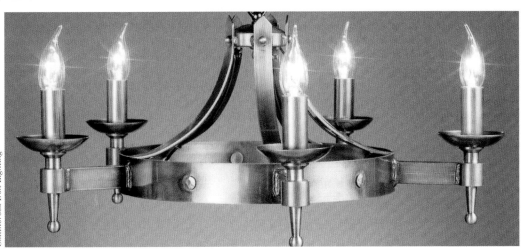

Smithbrook Iron Lighting

Smithbrook Iron Lighting

design for a candlestick, described in a letter to Hardman in 1848, would 'take light well and sparkle'.

Although he used gilded bronze for some of his candlesticks, the magnificent chandeliers he produced for the Palace of Westminster were all brass, and the one he designed for Alton Towers was of gilt, brass and crystal. He also exhibited a number of chandeliers at the Great Exhibition, including an octagonal one decorated with pinnacles and heraldic symbols, which were hailed as 'excellent examples of modern manufacture, unsurpassed in careful fabrication'.

Pugin also used wrought iron for lighting, and described one design for a simple corona (a circular chandelier) and some sconces as 'a crocket of iron with some pierced work and seven standards with plain pans'. These coronae were made either of pierced iron, which was later painted, or of pierced brass decorated with engravings or enamelwork.

Instead of using ecclesiastically shaped metalwork, which was soon being widely reproduced, Eastlake recommended a simple brass sliding ceiling pendant, which could be lowered or raised in order to provide the appropriate amount of light in a room. This kind of light was especially favoured in the dining room. He also suggested a design for a sconce and some gas brackets which he felt would enhance a tasteful domestic interior. He preferred brass for candlesticks, as opposed to the equally fashionable bronze, because it was 'more brilliant' and was 'capable of being beaten with greater richness of form and surface decoration' than other metals.

Large brass or wrought-iron chandeliers were well suited to the main rooms of a Gothic Revival house, even in a more modest villa, and were soon being copied by a number of manufacturers. Today, many can still be found, which can be converted to electricity for modern usage; while reproductions are also available from specialist firms.

As in other styles of Victorian home, a variety of types of illumination would be found together in one room, although more elaborately worked light fittings appeared in the public rooms, and simpler hanging lamps were placed in the bedrooms and other less important rooms of the house.

THIS PAGE: *Designs for metalwork lights and chandelier hooks. One of the hooks (bottom centre) was on display in the Medieval Court at the Great Exhibition, while the candelabrum (bottom right) was designed by Dresser.*

OPPOSITE: *The magnificent chandeliers designed by Pugin were inspired by some of these lamps and sconces, which were illustrated in his* Designs for Iron and Brasswork in the Style of the Fifteenth and Sixteenth Centuries.

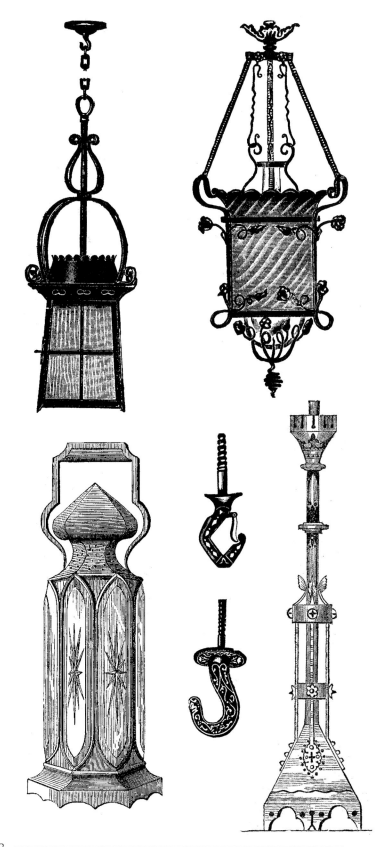

Chapter 6
The Revivalist Garden

'The modern [asymmetrical] style presents to you a constant change of scene perfectly in accordance with the desires of a man who loves as he continues to walk, to have new objects laid open to his view.'

Landscape gardener André Parmentier (1780-1830)

OPPOSITE: *Conservatories were a popular feature of Victorian homes and were built to complement the style of the building they abutted.*

BELOW: *Secluded areas in the Revivalist garden echoed the hortus conclusus of the medieval world.*

As mentioned in the Introduction, the Gothic Revival in the eighteenth century actually began in the garden, with temples, porticoes and faux medieval ruins being placed in the grounds of large landed estates to add interest to a view. These small, usually impermanent structures allowed landowners to experiment with the 'new' architectural style to see if they liked it. Batty Langley's *Ancient Architecture Restored and Improved* was highly influential in spreading the revival of Gothic forms by advising craftsmen and builders how to construct these ornamental buildings and how to restore medieval ones. Later Revivalists, however, would have agreed with Horace Walpole's caustic comment that 'the Goths never built summer houses or temples in a garden'.

The Victorian Revivalist garden adopted some eighteenth-century forms, but was also strongly influenced by nineteenth-century technological and botanical discoveries as well as by the growth of the middle classes, who, for the first time, had gardens of their own. Seeing the garden as yet another area to decorate and to display their wealth, they readily planted many of the exotic plants newly introduced into England from all over the world by travellers and horticulturalists; these were on display at the Royal Botanic Garden at Kew, and were flourishing in the new glass houses and conservatories made possible by innovations in the production of glass and ironwork.

As in architecture, the predominant Victorian style was the Italian garden with its symmetrical, formal plan and open prospect. The Revivalists, however, began looking back to the gardens of the Middle Ages and of the sixteenth and seventeenth centuries, and recreated the *hortus conclusus* – the garden secure and protected from the outside world. This emphasis on enclosure and seclusion – in what became known as the 'old-fashioned'

Vale Garden Houses Ltd

155

or 'old-world' garden – gained popularity by the 1860s and 1870s, with gardens being divided into areas by means of yew hedges and walls.

Other medieval features also appeared in the garden, with one villa in Stanmore, Hertfordshire, being described as having 'even the doors in the walls surrounding the kitchen-garden adorned with windows of coloured glass at the top, which had a singular and beautiful brilliancy among the foliage. The little flower-garden, too, was laid out in beds of gothic forms surrounded by gravel walks, and the fancy had not a bad effect.'

Traditional forms of planting were also revived, including herbaceous borders and orchards full of fruit trees. As Reginald Blomfield wrote in *Formal Garden in England* (1892): 'Nothing can be more beautiful than

some of the walks under the apple-trees in the gardens at Penshurst [in Kent]. Yet the landscape gardener would shudder at the idea of planting a grove or hedge of apple-trees in his garden. Instead of this he will give you a conifer or a monkey-puzzle ... Again, the pear-tree and the chequer-tree, the quince, the medlar, and the mulberry are surely entitled by their beauty to a place in the garden. It is only since nature has been taken in hand by the landscapist and taught her proper position that these have been excluded.' However, monkey-puzzle trees introduced from Chile in the 1840s did appear in the gardens of Gothic villas, and were also planted at Holly Village, the Gothic Revival estate built by Baroness Burdett-Coutts in north London in 1865.

Nostalgia for the natural environment influenced Gothic Revivalists in America, especially Andrew

Jackson Davis who wanted to restore the lost harmony of nature, which he felt had been devastated by the expansion of cities, railways, roads and canals across the landscape. His *Treatise on the Theory and Practice of Landscape Gardening* was published in 1841 and put forward a programme of national beautification. Like other Revivalists, his message also had a moral purpose, for he believed that a correctly designed house surrounded by a virtuous garden would act as 'an unfailing barrier against vice, immorality and bad habits'. In his attempt to harmonise architecture with nature, he echoed Thoreau's sentiments that 'man's works must lie in the bosom of Nature, cottages be buried in trees, or under vines and moss, like rocks, that they might not outrage the landscape'. Even the smallest cottage could have a perfect vista if it were properly placed in a position where it could catch a glimpse of a nearby wood or some other natural feature. However, with the growth of suburbia, Downing recognised that a formal approach was more suitable for the smaller gardens attached to the new urban villas, where irregularity was less appropriate.

John Claudius Loudon, who founded *The Gardeners' Magazine* in 1826, became an authority for the middle classes who were new to gardening. His *The Suburban Gardener or Villa Companion* (1838) divided gardens into geometric – or architectural – and natural types, with the latter being 'grounds and plantations formed in flowing lines' to emulate nature. Again, this irregular style, which Loudon split into Picturesque, Rustic and Gardenesque types, was more suitable for rural villas and country homes than for the rectangular plots

Although many estates had ornamental Gothic buildings in their grounds to break the view and provide a feature, smaller country houses could also place a pagoda, summer house or folly in the garden. Urban homes could add decoration to their gardens and boundaries with Gothic-style trelliswork, railings and gates, and Loudon's Gardening Encyclopaedia illustrated some of the appropriate styles that were available.

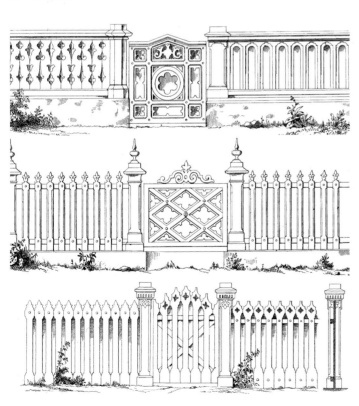

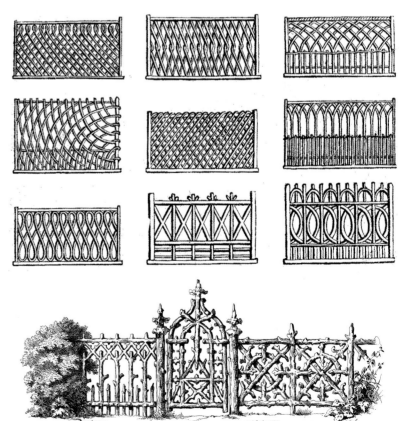

found with the new suburban houses, although rockeries and shrubberies provided a more natural element.

Rustic features could be added to a more formal garden by introducing newly available cast-iron garden seats with designs in the shape of fern fronds or intertwined branches, or trelliswork around arches and walls made from cast iron or wood.

Stone, wood and ironwork garden ornaments and benches were embellished with Gothic arches and mythical animals, while summer houses were designed with Gothic windows and other decorative details. Surrounded by wild-flower gardens or a small lake, they merged into the natural landscape. Highly ornamental exteriors and interiors made the conservatory an important additional room.

Vale Garden Houses Ltd

Vale Garden Houses Ltd

By the 1870s, the Arts and Crafts movement were repeating the call for a return to more natural gardens and for plants to be seen in their natural state. William Robinson in his magazine *The Garden*, first published in 1871, led this vogue for the 'wild garden', a style which recreated the old English cottage garden and was in the spirit of John Ruskin's and William Morris's philosophies. Wide lawns, informal beds, and romantic, delicately coloured herbaceous borders were features of his gardens, which also included natural paths of stone or grass.

Colour in the garden was important to both Robinson and his most important follower, Gertrude Jekyll. As Jekyll's partner, Edwin Lutyens, was to write, 'The true adornment of a garden lies surely in its flowers and plants. No artist has so wide a palette as the garden designer, no artist has greater need of discretion and reserve'. Jekyll was to continue and develop Robinson's natural style, becoming one of the most influential garden designers of the early twentieth century.

Conservatories

New technology and the growing interest in exploration and scientific discovery combined to make the conservatory, or garden room, a Victorian phenomenon, with even a modest home having one attached to the rear of the house. Developments in cast-iron production and in heating techniques, along with the wider availability of cheaper glass after the abolition of the window tax in 1851, allowed more people to afford these newly fashionable rooms, which were not only seen as an extra room to sit in, but were also ideally suited to house the wide variety of unusual plants and flowers being imported for the first time from all over the world.

Joseph Paxton's glass building, the Crystal Palace, which housed the 1851 Great Exhibition, harnessed the new techniques by using a ridge-and-furrow system of glazing supported by cast-iron columns, wrought-iron girders and timber. This structure, which was visited by thousands of people, inspired the wealthy middle classes to attach a conservatory to their home and to fill it with a selection of exotic plants, which would proclaim to the world how avant-garde they were. In Gothic Revival homes, where the living rooms were on the ground floor, the conservatory led off from the main reception rooms; in other styles of home the conservatory led off from the drawing room on the first floor. In all cases, however, the idea was for guests to be able to view the lavish greenery with admiration.

THIS PAGE AND OPPOSITE: Flower stands and bird tables were also ornately decorated, as these examples from Samuel Sloan's The Model Architect *show, while Loudon published drawings of conservatories filled with lush greenery, exotic plants and fountains.*

Also, with the growing interest in gardening, an occupation which the Victorians deemed suitable for ladies, conservatories were practical additions to the house, providing the right conditions to cultivate and nurture plants for the garden.

The design of a conservatory usually reflected the architecture of the house, and large panes of glass in the shape of Gothic arches were a popular style for the Gothic Revival garden room. These conservatories were filled with furniture as well as plants, including chairs and tables made from cast iron, wicker or wood, and decorative plant holders and urns, again in styles echoing the interior of the house; thus, floriated forms and other Gothic motifs soon found their way into the conservatory. Hard-wearing encaustic tiles paved the floors, while windows were often filled with stained-glass panes.

Today, conservatories in the Gothic style are being made by a number of specialist firms, while interesting antiques and garden ornaments can still be found to enhance their interiors.

STOCKISTS

The lists of suppliers given on these pages cannot be exhaustive and are intended only as a starting point. Local papers and commercial telephone directories are always worth looking at and are good sources of information about your own area. Alternatively, there are many organisations giving specialist information and advice, and others who will search for specific items.

ARCHITECTURAL ANTIQUES

Architectural Antiques
70 Pembroke Street
Bedford MK40 3RQ
Tel: 01234-213131

Architectural Rescue
1-3 Southampton Way
Camberwell
London SE5 7JH
Tel: 020-7277-0315

Cronin's Architectural
  Antiques
25 Arch Miles Street
off South Lambeth Road
London TW12 2JF
Tel: 020-7793-1499

Drummond's
  Architectural Antiques
The Kirkpatrick Bldgs
25 London Road
Hindhead
Surrey GU26 6AB
Tel: 01428-609444

Holyrood Architectural
  Salvage
The Tun Rooms
Holyrood Business Park
146 Duddingston Road W.
Edinburgh EH16 4AP
Tel: 0131-661-9305

The Original
  Architectural Salvage
  Co. Ltd
South Gloucester Street
Dublin 2, Eire
Tel: 00353-86-820770

Solopark Plc
Station Road
Pampisford
Cambridge
Cambs. CB2 4HB
Tel: 01223-834663

Walcot Reclamation
108 Walcot Street
Bath
Avon BA1 5BG
Tel: 01225-444404

BATHROOMS

Antique Baths of
  Ivybridge
Erne Bridge Works
Ermington Road
Ivybridge
Devon PL21 9DE
Tel: 01752-698752

Alscot Bathroom Co.
The Stable Yard
Alscot Park
Preston-on-Stour
Warks. CV37 8BL
Tel: 01789-450861

Au Temps Perdu
30 Midland Road
St Philip
Bristol
Avon BS2 0JY
Tel: 0117-929-9143

Catchpole and Rye
Posh Tubs
High Haden
Ashford
Kent TN26 3LY
Tel: 01233-80515
www.catchpolerye.co.uk

Chatsworth Bathrooms
  Ltd
10-12 Seddon Place
Stanley Industrial Estate
Stanley
Skelmersdale
Lancs. WN8 8EB
Tel: 01695-559874

Den of Antiquity
6 Wendell Road
London W12 9RT
Tel: 0181-354-4290

Dorset Reclamation
The Reclamation Yard
Cow Drove
Bere Regis
Dorset BH20 7JZ
Tel: 01929-472200

EASY Architectural
  Salvage
Unit 6, Couper Street
off Coburg Street
Leith
Edinburgh EH6 6HH
Tel: 0131-554-7077

Heritage Bathrooms Plc
Smallmead Road
Reading
Berks. RG2 OQS
Tel: 01118-931-3030

Ideal-Standard
The Bathroom Works
National Avenue
Kingston Upon Hull
Yorks. HU5 4HS
Tel: 01482-346461
www.ideal-standard.co.uk

Imperial Bathroom Co.
Imperial Buildings
Northgate Way
Aldridge
Walsall
W. Midlands WS9 8SR
Tel: 01922-743074

Light Innovation Ltd
362 Kingston Road
Ewell, Epsom
Surrey KT19 ODT
Tel: 020-8873-1582

Old Fashioned
  Bathrooms
The Forester's Hall
52 High Street
Debenham
Suffolk IP13 6QW
Tel: 01728-860926

Posh Tubs
Moriati's Workshop
High Halden, Ashford
Tenterden
Kent TN26 3LY
Tel: 01233-850155

Reclamation Services
Catbrain Quarry
Painswick Beacon
nr Stroud
Glos. GL6 6SU
Tel: 01452-814064

Shortland
Coachgap Lane
Langar
Notts. NG13 9HP
Tel: 01949-860121

Swiss Cottage Antiques
85 Westfield Crescent
Leeds
Yorks. LSA3 1DJ
Tel: 0113-242-9994

The Water Monopoly
16/18 Lonsdale Road
London NW6 6RD
Tel: 020-7624-2636

Woodstock Furniture
4 William Street
London SW1 9HL
Tel: 020-7245-9989

BEDROOMS

And So To Bed
638/640 King's Road
London SW6 2DU
Tel: 020-7731-3593
www.andsotobed.co.uk

Brass Knight Furnishing
Cumeragh House Farm
Cumeragh Lane
Whittingham, Preston
Lancs. PR3 2AL
Tel: 01772-786666

Deptich Designs Ltd
7 College Fields
Prince George's Road
London SW19 2PT
Tel: 0181-687-0867

The Guild of Master
  Woodcarvers
The Carp
Ruishton, Taunton
Somerset TA3 5JE
Tel: 01278-424246

The Hand-Crafted Bed
  Company Ltd
Lowdham House
Epperstone Road
Lowdham
Notts. NG14 7BU
Tel: 0115-9663800

Jonathan Tebbs
Abbey House
Eastfield Road
Louth
Lincs. LN11 7HJ
Tel: 01507-603173

Moss Brothers Metal
  Designs
26 Sunbury Workshops
Hocker Street
London E2 7LF
Tel: 020-7739-2361

Once Upon A Time
The Green
Ripley
Surrey GU23 6AL
Tel: 01483-211330

Seventh Heaven
Chirk Mill
Chirk
Wrexham County
Borough LL14 5BU
Tel: 01691-777622/773563
www.seventh-heaven.co.uk

Shortland
Coachgap Lane
Langar
Notts. NG13 9HP
Tel: 01949-860121

Sterling Wrought
  Ironworks
Unit 8
Angerstein Busness Park
Horn Lane, Greenwich
London SE10 ORT
Tel: 020-8305-1874

Trevor Lawrence
105/7 Station Road East
Oxtead
Surrey RH8 OAX
Tel: 01883-730300

Victorian Brass Bedstead
  Company
Hoe Copse
Cocking, nr Midhurst
West Sussex GU29 0HL
Tel: 01730-812287

Victorian Dreams
The Old Holme School
Crabtree Lane
Village Green
Hants. GU35 8QH
Tel: 01428-717000

DOORS & WINDOWS
Aladdin's Architectural
  Antiques
1 Shields Road, Byker
Newcastle-upon-Tyne
NE6 1FJ
Tel: 0191-265-3993

Batons to Beams
Unit 4, Pool Bank Park
High Street, Tarvin
Chester
Cheshire CH3 8JH
Tel: 01829-741900

Borders Architectural
  Antiques
2 South Road, Wooler
Northumberland
Tel: 01668-282475

Cardiff Reclamation
Site 7, Tremorfa
  Industrial Estate
Rover Way
Cardiff CF24 5SD
Tel: 029-2045-8995

In-Doors
Beechinwood Farm
Beechinwood Lane
Platt
nr Sevenoaks
Kent TN15 8QN
Tel: 01732-887445

Original Doors
  Save A Tree
93 Endwell Road
London SE4 2NF
Tel: 020-7252-8109

Ransford Bros
Drayton Way
Drayton Fields
Daventry
Northants. NN11 5XW
Tel: 01327-705310

DOOR FURNITURE
Arnold and Oakley
28 Kyle Street
Ross-on-Wye
Hereford HR9 7DB
Tel: 01989-567946

Ashfield Traditional
Forward Green
Stowmarket
Suffolk IP14 5HP
Tel 01449-711273

Brondesbury
  Architectural
  Reclamation
The Yard
136 Willesden Lane
London NW6 7TE
Tel: 020-7328-0829

Gnu
Old Bakery
Pontesbury
Salop SY5 0PY
Tel: 0800-163755

Mongers
15 Market Place
Hingham
Norwich
Norfolk NR0 4AF
Tel: 01953-851868

Stiffkey Antiques
The Old Chapel
Wells Road
Stiffkey
Norfolk NR23 1AJ
Tel: 01328-830099

The Victorian
  Ironmonger
The Old Garage
Broad Street, Fosseway
Brinklow
Warks. CV23 0LN
Tel: 01788-832292

Clayton Munroe Ltd
Kingston West Drive
Kingston, Staverton
Totnes
Devon TQ9 6AR
Tel: 01803-762626
www.clayton-munroe.com

**FLOOR/ENCAUSTIC
TILES**
H. & R. Johnston
Highgate Tile Works
Tunstall
Stoke-on-Trent ST6 4JX
Tel: 01782-575575

Original Features
155 Tottenham Lane
London N8 9BT
Tel: 020-8348-5155

Original Style
Falcon Road
Sowton Industrial Estate
Exeter
Devon EX2 7LE
Tel: 01392-474058

The Original Flooring
  Company
230A Grange Road
King's Heath
Birmingham B14 7RS
Tel: 0121-605 8898

Paris Ceramics Ltd
583 Kings Road
London SW6 2EH
Tel: 0171-371 7778

FIREPLACES
Antique Fireplace Centre
30 Molesworth Road
Millbridge
Plymouth
Devon PL1 5NA
Tel: 01752-559441

The Antique Welsh
  Slate Co.
Wervil Grange
Pentragat
nr Cardigan
Wales SA44 6HR
Tel: 07971-431695

Architectural Heritage of
  Northants.
Heart of the Shires
  Shopping Village
Brockhall
Northants. NN7 4LB
Tel: 01327-349249

Britain's Heritage
Shaftesbury Hall
3 Holy Bones
Leicester
Leics. LE1 4LJ
Tel: 0116-251-9592

Corallion Stone
  Reproductions
Hyde Lane
Hemel Hempstead
Herts. HP3 8SA
Tel: 01923-261767

Firecraft
1159 Melton Road
Syston, Leicester
Leics. LE7 2JS
Tel: 0116-269-7030

Frome Reclamation
Station Approach
Wallbridge
Frome
Somerset BA11 1RE
Tel: 01373-453122

LASSCo
St Michael's Church
Mark Street
London EC2A 4ER
Tel: 0171-7398-0448

Manorhouse Stone
School Lane
Normanton-le-Heath
Leicester
Leics. LE67 2TH
Tel:01530-262999

The Original Reclamation
  Trading Company
22 Elliot Road
Love Lane Industrial
  Estate
Cirencester
Glos. GL7 1YS
Tel: 01285-653532

R. & R. Renovations &
  Reclamation
Canalside Yard
Audlem
Cheshire CW3 0DY
Tel: 01270-811310

Robert Aagaard & Co.
Frogmire House
Stockwell Road
Knaresborough
North Yorks. HG5 0JP
Tel:01423-864805

Rococo Architectural
  Antiques
5 New Street
Lower Weedon
Weedon Bec
Northants. NN7 4QS
Tel: 01327-431288

Rudloe Stoneworks
Lower Rudloe Farm
Box, Nr Corsham
Wilts. SN13 0BP
Tel: 01225-811545
www.rudloe-stone.com

Stoneworks of Bath
108 Walcot Street
Bath
Avon BA1 5BG
Tel: 01225-311136

Stovax Ltd
Falcon Road
Souton Industrial Estate
Exeter
Devon EX2 7LF
Tel: 01392-474000

Symonds Salvage
Colts Yard
Pluckley Road
Bethersden, nr Ashford
Kent TN26 3DD
Tel: 01233-829724

Templestone
Station Wharf
Castle Cary
Somerset BA7 7PE
Tel 01963-350242
www.templestone.co.uk

Toby's Architectural
  Antiques
Station Road
Exminster
Devon EX6 8DZ
Tel: 01392-833499

Toby's Architectural
  Antiques
Brunel Road
Newton Abbot
Devon TQ12 4PU
Tel: 01626-351767

FURNITURE
Arthur Brett & Sons Ltd
Hellesdon Park Road
Drayton High Road
Norwich NR6 5DR
Tel: 01603-486633
www.arthur-brett.com/absweb/

Deacon & Sandys
Hillcrest Farm Oast
Hawkhurst Road
Cranbrook
Kent TN17 3QD
Tel: 01580-243331

Mark Wilkinson
Overton House
High Street, Bromham
nr Chippenham
Wilts. SN15 2HA
Tel: 01380-850004

Robert Mills Ltd
Architectural Antiques
Narroways Road
Eastville, Bristol
Avon BS2 9XB
Tel: 0117-955-6542

Steve Allen Originals
P. O. Box 51
Blackburn
Lancs. BB2 3GH
Tel: 01254-54146

Trevor Lawrence
105/7 Station Road East
Oxtead
Surrey RH8 OAX
Tel: 01883-730-0300

Thistle Joinery Ltd
77 Idleton Road
Bermondsey
London SE16 3JZ
Tel: 020-7232-5300

Victorian Wood Works
International House
L.I.F.T.
Temple Mills Lane
London E15 2ES
Tel: 020-8534-1000
victorianwoodworks.co.uk

GARDENS
Haddonstone
The Forge House
East Haddon
Northants. NN6 8DB
Tel: 01604-770711

Holloways
Lower Court
Suckley
Worcs. WR6 5DE
Tel: 01886-884665

Marston & Langinger
192 Ebury Street
London SW1W 8UP
Tel: 0171-824-8818

Oxleys Furniture
Lapsgone Farm
Westington Hill
Chipping Campden
Glos. GL55 6UR
Tel: 01386-840466

Saffron Oak
Saffron House
St John's Road
Hazelmere
Bucks. HP15 7QS
Tel: 01494-536618

Renzland Forge Ltd
London Road
Copford
Colchester
Essex CO6 1LG
Tel: 01206-210212

Vale Garden Houses Ltd
Melton Road
Harlaxton
nr Grantham
Lincs. NG32 1HQ
Tel: 01476-564433

KITCHENS
Brass & Traditional
    Sinks Ltd
Devauden Green
Chepstow
Mons. NP6 6PL
Tel: 01291-650738
www.sinks.co.uk

Chalon
The Plaza
535 Kings Road
London SW10 OSZ
Tel: 020-7351-0008
www.chalon.com

Mark Wilkinson
Overton House
High Street, Bromham
Nr Chippenham
Wilts. SN15 2HA
Tel: 01380-850004

Martin Moore
36 Church Street
Altringham
Cheshire WA14 4DW
Tel: 0161-928-2643

Robinson & Cornish Ltd
Southay House
Oakwood Close
Roundswell
Barnstaple
Devon EX31 3NJ
Tel: 01271-329300

Romsey Cabinetmakers
Unit 4
Greatbridge Business Pk
Budds Lane
Romsey
Hants. SO51 0HA
Tel: 01794-522626

Shortland
Coachgap Lane
Langar
Notts. NG13 9HP
Tel: 01949-860121

Smallbone of Devizes
105-109 Fulham Road
London SW3 6RL
Tel: 0171-589-5998

Smithbrook Ltd
Smithbrook
nr Cranleigh
Surrey GU6 8LH
Tel: 01483-272744

LIGHTING
Brooklands Brass
    Lighting
Smithbrook
nr Cranleigh
Surrey GU6 8OH
Tel: 01483-267-474

Christopher Wray
    Lighting
591-593 King's Road
London SW6 2YW
Tel: 020-7736-8434

Light Innovation Ltd
Ewell
Epsom
Surrey KT19 ODT
Tel: 020-8873-1582

Fritz Fryer Antique
    Lighting
12 Brookend Street
Ross-on-Wye
Hereford HR9 7EG
Tel: 01989-567416

Jeanne Temple Antiques
Stockwell House
Wavendon
Milton Keynes
Bucks. MK17 8LS
Tel: 01203-862-9333

Jim Lawrence
Traditional Ironwork
Scotland Hall Farm
Stoke by Nayland
Colchester
Essex CO6 4QG
Tel: 01206-263459
www.jim-lawrence.co.uk

Lamp Parts
High Street
Ramsbury
Wilts. SN8 2PA
Tel: 01672 -520454

Magic Lanterns at
    By George
23 George Street
St Albans
Herts. AL3 4ES
Tel: 01727-865680

Olivers Lighting
    Company
Udimore Workshops
Udimore
Rye
Kent TN31 6AS
Tel: 01797-225-166

W Sitch & Co.
48 Berwick Street
London W1V 4JD
Tel: 020-7437-3776

Smithbrook Ltd
Smithbrooke
Nr Cranleigh
Surrey GU6 8LH
Tel: 01483-272-744

PANELLING
Andy Thornton
    Architectural Antiques
Victoria Mills
Stainland Road
Greetland
Halifax
Yorks. HX4 8AD
Tel: 01422-377-314

Architectural
    Reclamation
Unit 1
Fforest Business Centre
Queensway
Fforestfach Industrial
    Estate
Swansea SA5 4DH
Wales
Tel: 01792-548-2222

Bylaw The Furniture
    Makers
Bylaw (Ross) Ltd
The Old Mill
Brookend Street
Ross-on-Wye
Hereford HR9 7EG
Tel: 01989-562356

Chancellors Church
    Furnishings
River Nook Farm
Sunnyside
off Terrace Road
Walton-on-Thames
Surrey KT12 2ET
Tel: 01932-252736

In-Situ Architectural
    Antiques
3 Worsley Street
Hulme, Manchester
Cheshire MI45 4LD
Tel: 0161-839-2010

Pew Corner
Artington Manor Farm
Old Portsmouth Road
Artington
Guildford
Surrey GU3 1LP
Tel: 01483-533-337

WALLPAPER
Akzo Bobel Decorative
    Coating
Crown House
Hollins Road
Darwen
Lancs. BB3 0BG
Tel: 01254-704-951

Alexander Beauchamp
Greenacre Mill
Farholme Lane
Stacksteads
Bacup
Lancs. OL1 0EZ
Tel: 01706-872-155

Cole & Son
Chelsea Harbour Design
    Centre
Lots Road
London SW10 0XE
Tel: 020-7376-4628

Interior Decorators &
    Designers Assn Ltd
1-4 Chelsea Harbour
    Design Centre
Lots Road
London SW10 0XE
Tel: 020-7580-5404

USA

ARCHITECTURAL MILLWORK

Allegherry Restoration
P. O. Box 18032
Morganstown
WV 26507
Tel: 304-594-2570

American Custom
  Millwork
3904 Newton Road
P. O. Box 3608
Albany
GA 31706
Tel: 912-888-3303

Anthony Wood Products
P. O. Box 1081
Hillsboro
TX 766-345
Tel: 254-582-7225

Architectural Detail in
  Wood
41 Parker Road
Shirley
MA 01464
Tel: 978-425-9026

Barewood Associates
106 Ferris Street
Brooklyn
NY 11231
Tel: 718-875-9037

Classic Architectural
  Specialities
3223 Canton Street
Dallas
TX 75226
Tel: 214-748-7149

Cumberland Woodcraft
10 Stover Drive
P. O. Drawer 609
Carlisle
PA 17013
Tel: 717-243-0063

Eton Architectural
  Millwork
1210 Morse Avenue
Royal Oak
MI 48067
Tel: 248-543-9100

Gingerbread Man
327-3 Industrial Drive
Placerville
CA 95667
Tel: 916-622-0550

House of Moulding
15202 Oxnard Street
Van Nuys
CA 91411
Tel: 818-781-5300

Mad River Woodworks
189 Taylor Way
P. O. Box 1067
Blue Lake
CA 95525-1067
Tel: 707-668 5671

Myers Restoration &
  Architectural Salvage
RFD 2
P. O. Box 1250
Clinton
ME 04927
Tel: 207-453-7010

Pagliacco Turnings &
  Millwork
P. O. Box 225
Woodacre
CA 94973
Tel: 415-488-4333

Rickwood Turning
98 NE 20 Street
Miami
FL 33127
Tel: 305-573-9142

Vintage Woodworks
Hwy 34 South
P. O. Box 39
MSC 3690
Quinlan
TX 75474-0039
Tel: 903-356-2158
www.vintagewoodworks.com

BATHROOMS

A-Ball Plumbing Supply
1703 W. Burnside Street
Portland
OR 97209
Tel: 800-228-0134

Affordable Antique Bath
  & More
333 Oak Street
P. O. Box 444
San Andreas
CA 95249
Tel: 209-754-1797

Bathroom Machineries
P. O. Box 1020
495 Main Street
Murphys
CA 95247
Tel: 209-728-2031

Country Plumbing
5042 Seventh Street
Carpinteria
CA 93013
Tel: 805-684-8685

Antique Hardware &
  Home
19 Buckingham
  Plantation Drive
Blufton
SC 29910
Tel: 843-837-09790

The Brass Knob
2311 18th Street NW
Washington DC 20009
Tel: 202-332-3370

Mac the Antique Plumber
6325 Elvas Avenue
Sacramento
CA 95819
Tel: 800-916-2284

Olde Good Things
124 West 24th Street
New York
NY 10011
Tel: 212-989-8041

Pinch of the Past
109 West Broughton
  Street
Savannah
GA 31401
Tel: 912-232-5563

United House Wrecking
535 Hope Street
Stamford
CT 06906
Tel: 203-348-5371

Urban Archaeology
143 Franklin Street
New York
NY 10013
Tel: 212-431-4646

Waterworks
29 Park Avenue
Danbury
CT 06810
Tel: 800 899-66757

**DOORS AND
WINDOWS**

Allied Window Inc.
2724 W. McMicken Ave.
Cincinnati
OH 45214
Tel: 800-445-5411
www.invisiblestorms.com

Artistic Doors & Windows
10 S. Inman Drive
Avenel
NJ 07001
Tel: 732-726-9400

Authentic Stained Glass
12824 Hwy 431
Suite G
Guntersville
AL 35976
Tel: 205-582-7848

Center Lumber Co.
85 Fulton Street
Paterson
NJ 075059
Tel: 973-742-8303

Combination Door Co.
1000 Morris Street
P. O. Box 1076
Fond du Lac
WI 54936-1076
Tel: 920-922-2050

Doors by Decora
3332 Atlanta Hwy
P. O. Box 3426
Montgomery
AL 36109
Tel: 334-277-7910

Door Furniture
Acorn
P. O. Box 31
Mansfield
MA 02048
Tel: 800-835-0121

Drums Sash & Door Co.
P. O. Box 207
Drums
PA 18222
Tel: 717-788 -3007

Fineman Doors
6215 1/2 Nita Avenue
Woodland Hills
CA 91367
Tel: 818-999-1631

H. J. Hardware Restoration
Al Bar Wilmette Platers
127 Green Bay Road
Wilmette IL 60091
Tel: 847-251-0187

L. H. Hobein & Son
160 Snelson Road
Marshall
NC 28753-8543
Tel: 828-649-3238

Midwest Architectural
  Wood Products
300 Trails Road
Eldridge
IA 52748
Tel: 319-285-8000

Old Wagon Factory
P. O. Box 1427
103 Russel Street
Clarksville
VA 23927
Tel: 804-374-5717

Restoration Supply Co.
736 Walnut Street
Royersford
PA 19468
Tel: 610-948-9200

Timberlane Woodcrafters
  Inc.
197 Wissahickon Ave.
North Wales
PA19454
Tel: 800-250-2221
www.timberlane-wood.com

Wood Window Workshop
839 Broad Street
Utica
NY 13501
Tel: 315-732-6755

Woodpecker Mfg
1010 N. Cascade
Montrose
CO 81401
Tel: 970-249-2616

Woodstone Co.
P. O. Box 223
Patch Road
Westminster
VY 05158
Tel: 802-722-9217

ENCAUSTIC TILES

Architectural Accents
27th Piedmont Road
Atlanta
GA 30305
Tel: 404-266-8700

Architectural Artifacts
20 S. Ontario
Toledo
OH 43602
Tel: 419-243-6916

Classic Ceramic Tile
124 Tiles Lane
E. Brunswick
NJ 08816
Tel: 732-390-7700

Country Floors
15 E. 16 Street
New York
NY 10003
Tel: 212-627-8300

Designs in Tile
P. O. Box 358
Mount Shasta
CA 96967
Tel: 530-926-2629
www.designsintile.com

Mission Tile West
853 Mission Street
S. Pasadena
CA 91030
Tel: 818-799-4595

Shep Brown Assoc.
24 Cummings Park
Woburn
MA 01801
Tel: 781-935-8080

FIREPLACES/STOVES
A. & M. Victorian
    Decoration
2411 Chico Avenue
S. El Monte
CA 91733
Tel: 626-575-0693

Classic Cookers
90-2793 Lower Barnett
    Hill
Montpelier
VT 05602
Tel: 802-233-3620

Florida Victorian
    Architectural Salvage
112 W Georgia Avenue
Deland
FL 32720
Tel: 904-234-9300

Haddonstone
201 Hell Pl.
Bellmawr
NJ 08031
Tel: 609-931-7011

Heatilator
1915 W Saunders Street
Mt Pleasant
IA 52641
Tel: 319-385-9211

Hazelmere Mantel
5422 176th Street
Suite 2
Surrey
BC V3S 4C3
Tel: 604-574-7814

Good Time Stove Co.
Tel: 888-282-7506
www.goodtimestove.com

Mantel Craft
41-45 Parkway Drive
Florence
AL 35630
Tel: 205-764-4178

Nevers Oak Fireplace
    Mantels
312 N Hwy 101
Encinitas
CA 92024
Tel: 760-632-5805
.
The Old House Parts Co.
24 Blue Wave Mall
Kennebunk
ME 04043
Tel: 207-985-1999
www.oldhouseparts.com

KITCHENS
Avalon Studios
116 Bridge Street
Narrowsburg
NY 12764
Tel: 914-252-3614

Blue Bell Kitchens
1104 Bethlehem Park
P. O. Box 371
Springhouse
PA 19477
Tel: 215-646 5442

Classic Cookers
90-2793 Lower Barnett
    Hill
Montpelier
VT 05602
Tel: 802-223-3620

Christopher Peacock
    Cabinetry
151 Greenwich Avenue
Greenwich
CT 06830
Tel: 203-862-9333

Crownpoint Cabinetry
153 Charlestown Road
Claremont
NH 03743
Tel: 800-999-4994
www.crown-point.com

Fine Woodworking
16750 White Stone Road
Boyds
MD 20641
Tel: 301-972-8806

LIGHTING
Authentic Designs
42a The Mill Road
West Rupert
VT 05776
Tel: 802-394-771

City Lights
2226 Massachusetts Ave.
Cambridge
MA 01240
Tel: 617-547-1490

Mica Lamp Co.
517 State Street
Glendale
CA 91203
Tel: 818-241-7227

King's Chandelier
P. O. Box 667
Dept 01
Eden
NC 27289
Tel: 336-623-6188
www.chandelier.com

Rejuvenation Lamp &
    Fixture Co.
2550 N W Nicolai St
Portland
OR 97210
Tel: 888-343-8548
www.rejuvenation.com

Roy Electric Co. Inc.
22 Elm Street
Westfield
NJ 07090
Tel: 908-317-4665
www.westfieldnj.com/roy

V. Michael Ashford
Evergreen Studios
6543 Alpine Drive
SW Olympia
WA 98512
Tel: 360-352-0694

IRON/METALWORK
Adornments for
    Architecture
307 Hollow Road
Staatsburg
NY 12580
Tel: 914-889-8390

Antique Hardware Store
43 Bridge Street, Dept PD
Frenchtown
NJ 08825
Tel: 210-996-4040

Architectural Iron Co.
P. O. Box 126
104 Ironwood Court
Milford
PA 18337
Fax: 717-296-4766

Capital Cresting
    Architectural Iron Co.
P. O. Box 126
Milford
PA 18337
Tel: 800-442-4766
www.capitalcrestings.com

Boyler's Ornamental Iron
4407 State Street
Bettendorf
IA 52722
Tel: 319-355-3707

Chelsea Decorative
    Metal Co.
9603 Moonlight Drive
Dept 0H1
Houston
TX 77096
Tel: 713-721-9200
www.thetinman.co

Custom Ironwork
P. O. Box 253
Union
KY 41091
Tel: 606-384-4122

Decorative Metal Ceilings
W. F. Norman Corporation
P. O. Box 323
Nevada
MI 64772
Tel: 800-641-4038

Vulcan Supply Corp.
P. O. Box 100
Westford
VT 05494
Tel: 802-878-4103

WALLPAPER/FABRICS
Alcott & Bentley Old
    House Store
918 Baxter Avenue
Louisville
KY 40204
Tel: 502-584-8660

Bradbury & Bradbury
P. O. Box 155-C3
Benicia
CA 94510
Tel: 707-746-1900
www.bradbury.com

Carter & Co.
Mt Diablo Handprints
541 Ryder Street
Vallejo
CA 94590
Tel: 707-554-2682

Classic Revivals
1 Design Center Pl.
Suite 545
Boston
MA 02210
Tel: 617-574-9030

Country Curtains
Dept 32099
Stockbridge
MA 01262
Tel: 800-876-6123

J. R. Burrows & Co.
P. O. Box 522
Rockland
MA 02370
Tel: 781-982-1812

Nancy Borden
Period Textile Furnishing
P. O. Box 4381
Portsmouth
NH 03801
Tel: 603-4367-4284

Sanderson NA
979 Third Avenue
Suite 409
New York
NY10002
Tel: 212-319-7220

INDEX

SELECT BIBLIOGRAPHY

Aldrich, Megan, *Gothic Revival* (Phaidon Press, 1994)

Atterbury, Paul, and Wainwright, Clive (eds), *Pugin: A Gothic Passion* (Yale University Press, 1994)

Banham, Joanna, Macdonald, Sally, and Porter, Julia, *Victorian Interior Design* (Cassell, 1991)

Barrett, Helena, and Phillips, John, *Suburban Style: The British Home, 1840-1960* (Macdonald Orbis, 1987)

Brooks, Chris, *The Gothic Revival* (Phaidon Press, 1999)

Clark, Kenneth, *The Gothic Revival* (John Murray, 1995 edn)

Cooper, Jeremy, *Victorian and Edwardian Décor* (Abbeville Press, 1987)

The Crystal Palace Exhibition Illustrated Catalogue (London 1851; facsimile edn, Dover Publications, NY, 1970)

Dixon, Roger, and Muthesius, Stefan, *Victorian Architecture* (Thames & Hudson, 1985)

Downing, A. J., *The Architecture of Country Houses* (1850; republished by Dover Publications, 1969)

Eastlake, Charles, *Hints on Household Taste* (1868; facsimile edn, Dover Publications, NY, 1969)

Eastlake, Charles, *A History of the Gothic Revival* (1872)

Gere, Charlotte, *Nineteenth-Century Decoration: The Art of the Interior* (Weidenfeld & Nicolson, 1989)

Girouard, Mark, *The Victorian Country House* (Yale University Press, 1979)

Jones, Owen, *The Grammar of Ornament* (1856; facsimile edn, Studio Editions, 1986)

Leopold, Allison Kyle, *Victorian Splendor: Re-creating America's 19th-Century Interiors* (Stewart, Tabori and Chang, 1986)

Miller, Judith and Martin, *Victorian Style* (Mitchell Beazley, 1997)

Moss, Roger W., and Winkler, Gail Caskey, *Victorian Interior Decoration: American Interiors 1830-1900* (Henry Holt & Co., NY, 1986)

Osband, Linda, *Victorian House Style: An Architectural and Interior Design Source Book* (David & Charles, 1991)

Pugin, A. C., *Gothic Ornaments Selected from Various Buildings in England and France* (1831; reprinted as *Pugin's Gothic Ornament: The Classic Sourcebook of Decorative Motifs by Augustus Charles Pugin*, Dover Publications, NY, 1987)

Pugin, A. W. N., *Designs for Iron and Brass Work in the Style of the Fifteenth and Sixteenth Centuries* (1836)

Pugin, A. W. N., *The True Principles of Pointed or Christian Architecture* (1841)

Pugin, A. W. N., *Floriated Ornament* (1849; facsimile edn, Richard Dennis, 1994)

Ruskin, John, *The Seven Lamps of Architecture* (1849)

Ruskin, John, *The Stones of Venice* (1853)

Scott, George Gilbert, *Remarks on Secular and Domestic Architecture* (1858)

Shaw, Edward, *The Modern Architect: A Classic Victorian Stylebook and Carpenter's Manual* (1864; facsimile edn, Dover Publications, 1995)

Sloan, Samuel, *The Model Architect* (facsimile edn entitled *Sloan's Victorian Buildings*, Dover Publications, 1980)

The Victorian Society Publications:
   No. 1 Doors
   No. 3 Fireplaces
   No. 4 Interior Mouldings
   No. 5 Wallcoverings
   No. 7 Brickwork
   No. 8 Paintwork
Wissinger, Joanna, *Victorian Details* (W. H. Allen & Co., 1990)

ACKNOWLEDGEMENTS
The publishers wish to thank the proprietors of Langley Castle Hotel in Hexham, Northumberland, and Rudlow Hall Hotel in Corsham, Wiltshire, for their kind permission to reproduce photographs of various furnishings and architectural features in this book.

PICTURE CREDITS
Except where credited, all pictures are the property of Pictures for Print. Half title and page 134 *Decorative Tiles throughout the Ages*, Hans Van Lemmen, Bracken Books; page 7 *Floriated Ornament*, A.W.N. Pugin; pages 11 and 15 The Bridgeman Art Library; pages 58 top right, 142 and 143 *Decorative Tile Designs*, Carol Belanger Grafton, Dover Publications Inc.; page 159 top left Matthew Mitchell.